The Awesome Book About God for Kids

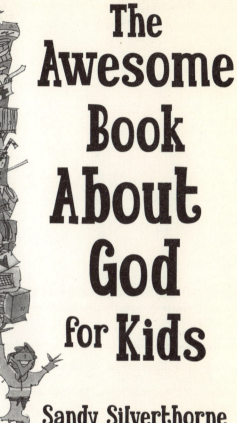

Sandy Silverthorne
Alisha Braatz

HARVEST HOUSE PUBLISHERS
EUGENE, OREGON

All Scripture quotations are taken from the Holy Bible, New Living Translation, copyright © 1996, 2004, 2007 by Tyndale House Foundation. Used by permission of Tyndale House Publishers, Inc., Carol Stream, Illinois 60188. All rights reserved.

Cover by Left Coast Design, Portland, Oregon

THE AWESOME BOOK ABOUT GOD FOR KIDS
Copyright © 2013 by Sandy Silverthorne and Alisha Braatz
Published by Harvest House Publishers
Eugene, Oregon 97402
www.harvesthousepublishers.com

Library of Congress Cataloging-in-Publication Data
   Silverthorne, Sandy
   The awesome book about God for kids / Sandy Silverthorne and Alisha Braatz
      pages cm
   ISBN 978-0-7369-5159-3 (pbk.)
   ISBN 978-0-7369-5160-9 (eBook)
   1. Bible stories, English. I. Title.
   BS551.3.S5483 2013
   220.95'05—dc23

                                      2013001168

Printed in the United States of America

     13 14 15 16 17 18 19 20 21 / BP-JH / 10 9 8 7 6 5 4 3 2 1

To Amelia and Paige

Contents

Contents

God Is My Defender & Protector

*The LORD spoke to Abram in a vision and said
to him, "Do not be afraid, Abram, for I will
protect you, and your reward will be great."*

GENESIS 15:1

Daniel and the Infamous Den of Hungry Lions

Daniel 6

When King Darius the Mede took control of Babylon, he chose three men to help him lead the country. He called them administrators and gave them great authority and power so they could supervise his interests and promote his royal command.

One of these three administrators was a Hebrew named Daniel who had come to Babylon as a young man. His education, professional capabilities, and special talents quickly earned the attention of King Darius. In fact, the king eventually decided to promote Daniel to be his second-in-command—a decision the other two administrators (whom we'll call Abban and Nigel) found utterly nauseating.

"Who does this guy think he is?" complained Abban. "What makes him so special?"

"He's not even Babylonian," Nigel said. "We should figure out how to get rid of him before he gets that promotion. We should be the ones getting raises, not him!"

"Right," said Abban. "We need a little dirt on Daniel."

That same day, Abban and Nigel began sifting through Daniel's trash, reading his mail, and secretly listening to his conversations—searching for anything they could bring before the king and criticize. But Daniel was responsible. He filed every document alphabetically and always checked everything twice. In addition, Daniel always told the truth! Always.

The next day, Abban resorted to stealing Daniel's calendar book, hoping Daniel would miss a few important meetings. But Daniel kept every appointment—and even arrived early! Abban was so frustrated he could have screamed.

"This isn't working!" Abban said. "Daniel is a real Goody Two-Shoes. There must be something else. Think, Nigel, think! Do you know anything about his religion?"

"Well," said Nigel, "I can only think of one thing. Every day during lunch, he goes home and opens his kitchen windows. Then, before he eats, he prays to his God. Could that be useful?"

"Yes!" Abban slapped Nigel on the back. "It's perfect. We'll make it illegal to pray to anyone but King Darius, and then we'll trap Daniel. The king will love the new law—you know how vain he is!"

"So what will happen to those who pray to their own gods?" asked Nigel.

"They'll be thrown into the Infamous Den of Hungry Lions!"

"The Infamous Den of Hungry Lions?" Nigel's eyes twinkled. "Where the bones of a thousand men are gnawed on day and night? How gruesome...it's perfect!"

That afternoon Abban and Nigel presented King Darius with their new idea. Just as they had predicted, he loved it.

"You mean everyone will bow to me? Whenever I say the word?" asked the king.

"Of course, divine King! That's the whole point," said Abban.

King Darius smiled broadly as he signed his name to the new law and sealed it with his signet ring. He ordered his messengers to spread 400 copies of the document throughout Babylon immediately so that everyone would be informed without delay. Then King Darius hurried to his dressing room to change into his silk robe with the ermine collar—the perfect outfit in which to be worshipped.

The "bow before me" law (as it was already being called) arrived on Daniel's desk just before lunch. He unrolled the scroll and began reading through the new statute. His shoulders sagged as its meaning sunk in. He surmised that its true authors were Abban and Nigel...who else would write such a senseless law? *Oh well*, Daniel thought, *nothing can be done now*. King Darius had approved the document with his own royal seal. Heartsick, Daniel slowly rolled up the scroll, filed it in its proper place, and set off for home.

After making a grilled cheese sandwich, Daniel did what he did every day—he bowed his head in thanks to God for a good meal, a steady job, and such beautiful weather. Underneath his open window, he heard an excited gasp.

"Gotcha!"

Daniel opened his eyes. Nigel stood on the sidewalk below, pointing at Daniel. "That's him! Praying to his God! Get him, boys— he'll be lion meat tonight!"

Sixteen royal guards barreled through Daniel's door, knocking over his kitchen table and trampling his grilled cheese sandwich into a crumbly grease spot on the floor. They tied Daniel's hands behind his back, pushed him down his stairs, and marched him straightaway to the prison. Meanwhile, Nigel ran as fast as he could back to the palace, breathlessly calling for an audience with the king. Abban was already sitting at the king's lunch table (enjoying a tuna sandwich on rye) when Nigel was ushered in.

"Nigel!" greeted the king, "come in, sit down. Have a Cheez-It!" He slid the crackers toward Nigel.

"In a moment, dear King," Nigel said in his most pathetic voice. "But first...I've run here as fast as I could. Did I misunderstand you this morning? Didn't you enact a new law? And hasn't that law already been circulated throughout the kingdom?"

"Indeed!" said King Darius. "That's why I'm wearing this robe." He fluffed up the ermine collar so that each hair stood on end. "Why? Would you like to worship me?"

"Of course!" said Nigel, "But first, we've got a problem, King Darius. One of your own staff members has just been caught in full defiance of your new decree!"

"Really? An employee? Who wouldn't like my law?" asked the king, putting down his sandwich.

"Daniel," said Nigel. "He has defied you. He chose to pray to his own God rather than you. I witnessed it myself!"

Abban pushed himself back from the table in mock disgust. "Daniel? Our fellow administrator? I can't believe it! How rude! How loathsome!"

"I know!" said Nigel. "It's hard to believe. I just wanted to let you both know before Daniel was thrown to the lions tonight."

"Wait!" shouted King Darius. "Are you sure you have the right man? You're talking about Daniel, my most trusted advisor?"

"That's him."

"Daniel..." said King Darius thoughtfully. "He's a Hebrew. He worships God, and...well, I never thought about what the new law would mean to him."

King Darius's forehead squished together. Minutes passed. Then he looked up hopefully. "We can't throw Daniel into the Infamous Den of Hungry Lions—he's a foreigner!"

"That's true," said Abban, "but the law specifically includes foreigners, and of course, the law of the Medes and Persians cannot be changed."

"B...b...but," said King Darius, "he can't be thrown to the lions because we're friends! I said so, and I'm the king!"

"I'm afraid friends count too."

King Darius burst into tears as Abban and Nigel marched out of the lunchroom and toward the prison. King Darius cried over his tuna sandwich and Cheez-Its until they were soggy and uneatable. He pushed his plate away and called for a box of Kleenex. One wasn't enough. King Darius used up six more boxes of tissue, crying through an afternoon choir performance, a tiger-taming show, and his four o'clock snack. Minutes before the dinner bell, he managed to pull himself together.

"Bring Daniel to me," he commanded, patting his swollen eyes with a cold washcloth.

Daniel was led into the king's throne room between two heavily armed guards and seated opposite the ruler.

"All afternoon," blubbered the king, "I've tried to think of ways to save you from the Infamous Den of Hungry Lions, but I haven't come up with anything. I never thought about you being eaten alive! How will I ever replace you?" He blew his nose into a napkin. "I just want you to know I'm rooting for you. May your God, whom you worship, rescue you." He put out his hand. "But just in case He doesn't...goodbye."

"Thank you, King Darius," replied Daniel as he shook the king's hand. Right away, guards lifted Daniel off his feet and carried him straight out of the palace and through the animal menagerie. When they reached the foul-smelling Infamous Den of Hungry Lions, they threw Daniel inside. The huge cats howled with pleasure, their orange eyes glowing in the dim light.

That evening, King Darius had a stomachache. He couldn't eat his steak dinner. He didn't enjoy any of the jugglers or cartwheeling monkeys at the after-dinner show. All he could think about was his friend Daniel. Even the harpist he called for did nothing but keep him awake. All night long he thought about the new law and how it had affected his friend. Finally he concluded that Abban and Nigel had certainly duped him into creating the treacherous scheme.

At the first glimmer of daylight, King Darius pushed the sleepy harpist out of the way and ran down the palace corridor.

"It's morning!" he shouted, "Everybody up! To the lions' den! Hurry!"

Out the door and down the path ran King Darius until he came to the Infamous Den of Hungry Lions. The stench of rotting meat flowed from the cavernous hole, prompting the king to hold his nose in disgust as he shouted, "Daniel! Are you alive? Did your God rescue you?"

A small voice called back, "Of course my God rescued me! I'm innocent, O King! I would not wrong you. My God sent an angel to shut the lions' mouths—they lay here and purred all night."

"Amazing!" cried King Darius. "Guards, open the door and let Daniel out!"

Immediately, the door was opened and Daniel walked out unscathed—but very, very stinky.

Later that morning, Abban and Nigel were arrested. They had tricked the king into throwing Daniel into the Infamous Den of Hungry Lions, so they were given the same treatment themselves.

Unfortunately for the two con men, the lions were now ravenous and made quick meals of them.

King Darius issued a new proclamation to his kingdom. "Good citizens of Babylon! Do you know the God of Daniel? He is the true God. His rule is never ending, He is a protector and defender of His children, and everyone should worship Him! He has rescued Daniel from the lions' den!"

God Is My Defender & Protector

Betrayed by his coworkers and set up to fail, Daniel didn't have a lot to be confident in—except his God. He believed God could defend and protect him, even in the Infamous Den of Hungry Lions.

Let Daniel's story inspire you. Stand up for God, and He'll stand up for you!

2

God Is
the Best Listener

*When you pray, I will listen. If you look for
me wholeheartedly, you will find me.*

JEREMIAH 29:12-13

Hannah's Request
1 Samuel 1–2

Hannah always wanted to be a mother. At school, other girls said they wanted to be hair stylists or to study medicine or to be veterinarians...but not Hannah. She only wished for a loving husband and a houseful of kids. After school, she practiced making peanut butter and jelly sandwiches and managing a home. She even diapered the family pigs, and she was so good at it that neighboring mothers asked her to show them how to do it too!

When Hannah grew up, she married the love of her life, Elkanah. Hannah expected her dream of motherhood was about to come true, but it didn't.

"Hannah, you are so ugly!" said Penny. "That's probably why you can't have a baby!" The hurtful words stung like a slap across the cheek. "Or maybe God doesn't think you'd be a very good mother," Penny added.

Usually, Hannah could shake off the mean remarks and walk away as if she didn't care. But not today. She dropped her basket of eggs and covered her face with both hands so Penny couldn't see her tears. Devastated, Hannah ran to the only place she knew she could be alone. She wanted to call on the Lord without Penny's spiteful comments or other people's prying eyes.

Hannah burst through the front doors of the synagogue and didn't stop running until she was at the front of the empty sanctuary. She dropped to her knees at the altar and began to pray silently.

Please, Lord, hear my prayer! I know my husband loves me and doesn't think I'm ugly. But, Lord, why can't I have a baby? I want to be a mother so badly. Please help me have a child. If You do, I promise...I promise I'll dedicate him back to You.

While she was praying, someone touched her back. "Miss," said the pastor, "the synagogue isn't open right now." He took one of Hannah's trembling hands and helped her stand.

"You look tired—or are you upset? Did you have a late night? Either way, you should really go home. This isn't the place to make a scene." The elder attempted to steer her down the aisle of the church. "Here, let me help you—"

"What?" said Hannah. "You don't understand! I'm praying! I've been pouring my heart out to God!" She wiped her runny nose on her sleeve. "Only God can answer my prayer—that's why I'm here."

"Then tell me, what's wrong?"

"My heart is broken. All my life I've wanted only to be a mother," said Hannah. "I just *know* I was meant to be one! I've married a wonderful man who will be a fantastic father, but somehow we cannot have a baby, and Penny, this other girl..." Hannah began crying again. "This other girl keeps telling me that I'm too ugly and that God doesn't think I'd be a good mother and that's why God hasn't let me have children! She's just so mean..." Hannah trailed off. "It's not true, is it?"

"Not even a little bit," said the elder. "Not even a smidgen. I think you've come to the right place after all. Let's pray together. May God grant you a baby!"

The man took both of Hannah's hands in his, and they bowed their heads. A quiet peace came over Hannah as she asked God for a miracle baby. As they said amen together, a new confidence grew in her heart. God had heard her prayer—she was sure of it!

Renewed, Hannah thanked the man and wiped her eyes. She left the synagogue with a smile on her face. Penny was no match for God!

Later that year, Hannah gave birth to a beautiful baby boy. She and Elkanah named him Samuel and dedicated him to the service of the Lord.

God Is the Best Listener ~~~~~~~~~~

Hannah's story teaches us the importance of our words. When you talk, God listens. When you whisper, He hears you! Even if you mumble, He still understands.

God wants to hear from you! Tell Him what's on your heart today.

~~~~~~~~~~~~~~~~~~~~~

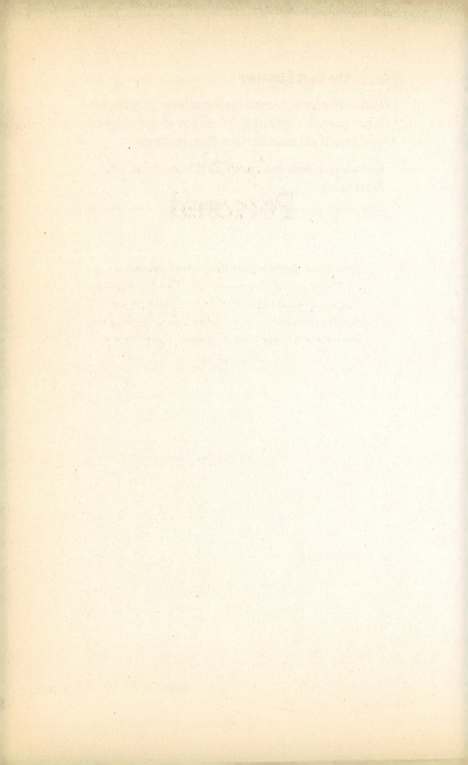

3

God Is
Personal

*Listen to me, descendants of Jacob, all you who remain in
Israel. I have cared for you since you were born. Yes, I carried
you before you were born. I will be your God throughout
your lifetime—until your hair is white with age. I made you,
and I will care for you. I will carry you along and save you.*

Isaiah 46:3-4

Zacchaeus Climbs a Tree
Luke 19

Zacchaeus made a new name badge for himself when he was promoted to chairman of the Jericho Tax Department. The gold-rimmed, oversize name tag glittered in the sunlight when he made his rounds through the city market.

Zacchaeus always greeted the business owners curtly, sticking out his chest to show off his badge. He made sure everyone knew about his promotion and newfound power. No longer would anyone joke about his height as they had before! If they did, they paid—with money! Even pretending to jest about his height could cost business owners a bundle of cash.

"Did you just look down at me?" Zacchaeus would ask. "I think you did! You looked at me funny! Think I'm short, huh? Well, that will cost you a thousand dollars!"

Zacchaeus made up the fines and didn't keep records of them. He pocketed the cash with a smirk and piled the money in his guest room, which was so full he could only crack the door to throw more inside.

One Thursday afternoon Jesus came to town. The streets of Jericho buzzed with His arrival. In fact, He'd already healed a blind man on His way through the city

24

gates! Market stalls closed, and people left work early to see Jesus, hear Him preach, and maybe see another miracle.

Intrigued, Zacchaeus listened to his neighbors discuss Jesus's arrival.

"Have you heard Him teach?" asked one. "He's full of God's power and wisdom!"

"It's true," agreed another. "He changed my life."

"And the miracles!" continued the first man. "He heals disease, forgives sin, and makes the winds and waves die down. He truly is the Son of God."

Son of God? thought Zacchaeus. *This Jesus might be a good person to know! With His influence, I might get another promotion!* And so Zacchaeus decided to follow the crowd. He would introduce himself to Jesus when the opportunity presented itself.

Zacchaeus imagined how the conversation would go. *Jesus, my name is Zacchaeus. You might have heard of me. Yes, that's right, chairman of the Jericho Tax Department. We should have dinner while You're in town. We could discuss Your tax status. I'd love to point out some loopholes Your accountant might have missed.* Zacchaeus checked himself in his hall mirror and straightened his shiny name badge. *Yes, Jesus will be glad to have me as a friend!*

Zaccheus left his home and started to hurry down the street, but the road was soon choked with people. He tried to push his way through, but no amount of sneaking, wriggling, or poking around the edges of the crowd got him any farther.

Dejected, Zaccheus stepped aside and assessed the situation. How would he ever get through? He simply had to meet Jesus...and that's when he had a brilliant idea. While everyone else mobbed Fillmore Street, he would run down Sycamore Alley and climb the tree at the three-way stop—right above where Jesus would pass!

Zaccheus bolted down Sycamore Alley and ran for the tree, hauling himself up on a branch moments before the huge crowd spilled into the intersection.

He spotted Jesus near the front of the procession and estimated that the best time to call down would be—

"Zaccheus!" Jesus called out, looking directly into Zaccheus's astonished face.

"Sir?" replied Zaccheus.

"Zaccheus, come down out of that tree. How silly of you! I'm coming to your house today for dinner. You're ready, aren't you?"

The crowd hushed.

"Well, uh...yeah," murmured Zaccheus, struggling to remove

himself from the fanning branches. "Just one moment, and I'll be—"

"Hey, Jesus!" hollered a man in the crowd, "Why would You eat with that scumbag?"

Others people shouted their disapproval as well.

"Good-for-nothing bureaucrat!"

"What a meanie! He skims off the top!"

Zacchaeus dropped out of the tree in front of Jesus. He brushed himself off and began to pull out his business card, but he put it back slowly as he heard the growing unrest around him.

"That Zacchaeus is nothing but a liar and cheat!"

"A lowlife who charges fake taxes!"

Zacchaeus turned a deep red as Jesus stood near him and listened to the people's comments. Was Jesus looking straight through him?

Normally Zacchaeus would levy an immediate "just because I can" tax on his detractors, reminding them who was in charge. But under Jesus's honest gaze, his mouth felt dry and he couldn't say the words. His name badge began to feel awfully heavy on his jacket. He quietly slipped it into his pocket and looked at the ground, embarrassed.

The crowd began to close in. "This cheater needs to be taught a lesson!"

"Watch your wallet, Jesus!"

"He's nobody's friend!"

"Now, hold on," said Jesus to the crowd, holding up His hands. He turned to Zacchaeus. "Is what they say true?"

Zacchaeus shuffled his feet across the sandy street. He felt very, very small—even smaller than he already was. "Maybe," he whispered. "Perhaps."

Jesus put a hand on his shoulder. "Zacchaeus, look at Me."

Zacchaeus looked up. Jesus's eyes were kind, and He did not condemn him like the rest of the crowd.

"Yes, it's all true!" burst Zacchaeus. "Everything they have said is true. I cheat. I steal. I lie! But Master, I can change! And I can start today." The words felt so good coming out of his mouth, Zacchaeus couldn't stop. He looked at his neighbors' angry faces and pointed at each one.

"John, I owe you two thousand dollars, but I will pay you four thousand! And William, I overtaxed your business by three percent last quarter. I'll make it up with change! Lucinda, I know you weren't talking about me in the market. I shouldn't have given you that fake fine. I'm going to repay you with interest!" Zacchaeus spread his arms wide. "Friends, today I am going to give half of my wealth to the poor! And to all of you whom I've overcharged, I'll pay you back four times what I've stolen!"

"Excellent," said Jesus, slapping him on the back. "Salvation has come to your home today!" Then He addressed the crowd. "This is why the Son of Man came—to seek and save the lost!"

A rumbling of discord passed over the mob of people. They didn't know what to make of Zacchaeus's new promises. Would he really pay them back?

"I'll do it! I really will!" said Zacchaeus, answering the people's unspoken question. "Everyone will be paid back what I owe—and more. In fact...everyone come to my home for dinner. Let me make it right this very night!"

It was quite a dinner.

God Is **Personal**

God desires a personal relationship with each one of His children. Every one! And He knows *everything* about you. He even knew you before you were born! He knows your name, where you live, who your parents are, and whether you'll need glasses next year. He knows all the good parts and all the bad parts...and He loves you anyway.

Zacchaeus didn't know he was going to meet the Savior when he left home that morning, but when he did, it changed his whole life. God wants to be friends with you. That's how important you are to Him.

4

God
Heals

I am the LORD who heals you.

EXODUS 15:26

As the sun went down that evening, people throughout the village brought sick family members to Jesus. No matter what their diseases were, the touch of his hand healed every one.

LUKE 4:40

Healing Faith
Luke 8

Serephina felt helpless. She had been sick for twelve years.

Twelve years she'd endured teasing and ridicule for a problem that medicine couldn't solve. Doctors' treatments didn't help. The yoga positions weren't doing any good. The vitamins, minerals, and salt baths hadn't cleared up her condition even a little bit.

It seemed so cruel that something she couldn't help should prevent her from being a part of the community. Hopeless and out of options, Serephina gave up. She stopped brushing her hair, stopped saying hello to neighbors at the market, and stopped trying to fit in.

The produce market bustled with activity every Tuesday morning. As always, Serephina shrugged off the cold glances and settled on whatever vegetables she could reach easily. She threw a package of figs in her basket, followed by three lemons and a bundle of asparagus, and hastily paid for her purchases.

On her way home, she found herself walking behind two former grade-school friends, Magna and Beatrice. She kept a respect-able distance, but she could still easily overhear their discussion.

"He's coming to town, you know!"

"Who is?"

"The Teacher...the Healer—Jesus!"

"Really? Jesus? I've heard He can heal all kinds of diseases."

"Yep, last week He told a paraplegic, 'Stand up and walk,' and he did! Maryanna, Felipe, and I thought we'd go hear His teaching this afternoon. Want to come?"

Beatrice and Magna turned the corner.

Serephina's heart pounded. Jesus the Healer would be in her town today! The Healer! A glimmer of hope stirred in her heart. *Maybe Jesus can heal me!* She walked faster, imagining a life without sickness: ice cream socials, barn parties, outdoor music festivals...she'd do it all!

But Serephina's cheerful daydreams ended as soon as she opened her front gate. Sighing, she picked up the stray garbage people had tossed in her yard, and she kicked a dirt clod off her front porch—daily reminders that she wasn't welcome in her hometown. She didn't want to hope for a miracle, only to be let down. Already the outcast, she didn't want yet another defeat, another disappointment.

Still, she thought, *if He truly has the power of God in Him, He can heal anyone. Even me!* She repeated those two last words as she unlocked her door and went inside to put away her groceries. *Even me. If only I can touch the hem of His robe, then surely I'll get well!*

Later that day, the crowds swelled around Jesus and His disciples as they left Matthew's house. People shouted and pushed their way to the center of the mob, requesting miracles for themselves and their family members.

Jesus answered as many people as He could while still trying to make His way down the street to His next appointment. Suddenly He stopped, scanning the crowd as if looking for someone He knew.

"Who touched Me?" He asked.

Silence blanketed the crowd. Lots of people had been jostling up against Jesus. Which one did He mean?

Serephina trembled. She ducked her head, retreating under people's arms and shoulders. Somehow she knew that Jesus had felt her touch—even though her fingers had barely grazed the hem of His coat. Afraid of added attention and inevitable ridicule, she pulled her scarf around her face even tighter.

"Serephina."

Stunned, Serephina raised her eyes. Jesus was looking right at her! "Your faith has made you well." She couldn't breathe. *The Healer is talking to me? He said that I've been made well?*

"Even me, Lord?" she asked.

Jesus nodded.

Surrounded by hundreds of townspeople, Serephina felt the loving attention of only one. She believed.

A moment later, Jesus was pulled away by His disciples. Two messengers were pushing through the people and shouting for His immediate attention. As Serephina turned to go home, the amazed crowd parted to let her through. Neighbors who had been standoffish now bowed their heads and respectfully reached out to touch her.

"Serephina!" called Beatrice. "You've been healed!" Beatrice put her hand out and patted Serephina gently on the shoulder.

"You're well!" said Magna, appearing out of the crowd of faces. Felipe and Maryanna also added well-wishes and congratulations.

Tears of gratitude welled up in Serephina's eyes. She motioned awkwardly to old acquaintances before escaping down an empty street. Once alone, she recounted her joyous meeting with the Savior and praised God out loud.

Then she gathered her skirts and ran home through the dusty streets, not caring whether she made a spectacle of herself. Some people might never understand, but others would welcome her back into the community wholeheartedly. Jesus had cured her, of that she was sure—and this was the first day of her new life, healed and made whole.

God Heals

Throughout history, God has been described as the Great Physician. In fact, much of Jesus's ministry focused on healing. God is our Creator, so He knows how we are made inside and out. Whether we have a physical ailment or a spiritual pain, God is the first physician we can call on for healing. No heart is too hurt, no scratch too small, no disease too complicated for our God.

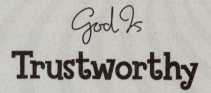

5

Trustworthy

Jesus told him, "I am the way, the truth, and the life."

<small>JOHN 14:6</small>

Even if everyone else in the world is a liar, God is true. As the Scriptures say about him, "You will be proved right in what you say, and you will win your case in court."

<small>ROMANS 3:4</small>

It's the Truth!

Luke 1

During the reign of Herod, king of Judea, a priest named Zechariah served in the temple of the Lord. He lived an honorable life, as did his wife Elizabeth. They kept all the commandments, attended the synagogue regularly, and loved God with all their hearts. Life couldn't have been better...except for one thing. Zechariah and Elizabeth had no children. Now that they were both very old with white hair and wrinkles, their daily prayer for a baby sounded more like a memorized script and less like a heartfelt desire.

As a priest, Zechariah had the opportunity to burn incense inside the sanctuary of God one time. Not one time per day, or one time per week, but one time in his whole life. When it was announced that his turn had finally arrived, he couldn't help but do a quick fist pump in the air before racing home to tell Elizabeth the news. She beamed with pride for her husband. It was the pinnacle of a priest's career!

"So when exactly will this happen?" she said, flipping open the family calendar.

"Well," said Zechariah, "I believe they said two weeks from today."

Elizabeth circled the calendar square in bright red ink with lightning bolts shooting off the date and wrote "BIG DAY!" Then she began writing a list of all the things to do beforehand: wash and iron their best clothes, clean the whole house, plan a menu for the celebratory dinner…it was a very long list.

As the big day approached, Elizabeth double-checked the last-minute preparations.

"Did you make an appointment to get your hair cut?" she asked Zechariah. "You don't want to look sloppy in the temple tomorrow."

"Yes, dear," replied Zechariah. "Today at four."

"What about your eyebrows? Do they need trimming? Here, look at me…" Elizabeth turned his face from side to side, inspecting him. "What about your fingernails—are they trimmed? Did you oil your good leather sandals? What about your temple robe? Shall I iron it again for you?"

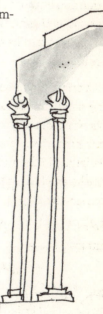

"Oh, Elizabeth," said Zechariah. "Don't worry about me." He hugged her tight, glad she cared so much. "Everything is perfect." Zechariah tried to sound extra confident even though his insides churned. Tomorrow was the biggest day of his life.

Early the next morning, Zechariah went up the stairs to the entrance of the Most Holy Place. Behind him, his family and friends gathered in the temple courtyard. They started praying and wouldn't stop until he had finished burning the incense before the Lord.

Alone at the altar, Zechariah mentally ran through the official procedures. He struck a match and watched the light bounce across the walls. The gold designs on the walls sparkled. The wood inlays glowed warmly. An angel of the Lord stood near...wait, what? An angel of the Lord?

Zechariah stood paralyzed with fear.

"Don't be afraid, Zechariah," said the angel. "God has heard your prayer. Elizabeth is going to have a baby boy—you're going to be a father!"

Zechariah's mouth fell open, and he gulped the air like a fish out of water. The match he held fell from his fingers and extinguished itself on the floor.

"Be happy!" continued the angel, smiling. "This is good news! Everyone is going to leap for joy when your little boy is born. He will be a very godly man. His name will be John."

The angel paused to let the words sink in.

"Your son will be special. He should never drink wine or beer. Instead, he's going to be filled with the Holy Spirit. He will be a mighty prophet, turning people back to God and serving the Lord with energy and excitement. So, what do you think?"

"Think?" stumbled Zechariah, finally finding his voice. "I'm

flabbergasted! First of all, an angel
has just met me in the Most
Holy Place! And then, this
angel tells me that I'm going
to be a father? Now, at my age?
What about Elizabeth? She is far
too old! How could we possibly be
parents at this point in our lives?"

The smile on the angel of the Lord's
face disappeared. He leaned over and put his face inches from
Zechariah's face, nose to nose.

"Don't you know who I am?" said the angel. "I'm Gabriel! I've come
directly from God's throne room to bring you this good news.
How could you question my message? How dare you doubt God's
will!" Gabriel's sword scraped across the floor as he leaned over
Zechariah's wilting frame. "You know what? Just for that...no
more talking! That's right! I don't want to hear another negative
word. What God says stands firm. His message is always true!
So I'm sorry, Zechariah, but you won't be speaking again until
this baby is born." Gabriel stood up to his full height and re-
adjusted his sword belt. "Everything I've said is factual and from
the mouth of God!"

And with that, Gabriel disappeared.

"Wait—" The word stuck in Zechariah's throat, unformed. His lips
and tongue were frozen and immobile. *I can't even whisper!* Shaking, Zechariah teetered back and forth in his good leather sandals.
After a good ten minutes, he unsteadily struck a second match,
lit the incense, and performed the ritual ceremony. Meanwhile,
he replayed Gabriel's visitation repeatedly in his mind. What on
earth will Elizabeth say when she finds out? What will the other
priests say? How will I explain what happened?

Outside in the courtyard, Elizabeth twisted her handkerchief. Behind her, the restless congregation awaited Zechariah's return, mumbling and whispering among themselves. When he finally appeared, everyone leaned forward for an explanation, straining to hear any special message from the priest.

Zechariah said nothing. Instead, he stood before the people waving his hands up and down, gesturing wildly. But no one could understand him!

"What is he saying?"

"I can't quite hear him, can you?"

"Not a word! It looks like he's playing charades."

"Charades? A party game? Now?"

A second priest rushed up the stairs to address the congregation. "He must have seen a vision! God has surely given him a message!"

The congregation's murmurs swelled as the second priest directed the excited Zechariah down the stairs and through a side door into the temple.

Elizabeth fainted.

~

Hours later, Zechariah arrived home. He tromped inside, shaking off pestering family members and waving them away. He needed to see Elizabeth. Alone.

Zechariah found her in bed with a cold compress on her forehead. He sat on the edge of the bedspread and squeezed her hand.

Elizabeth opened her eyes and peeked out from beneath the cold washcloth. "Thank goodness you're home," she said. "What on earth happened? Did you really see a vision?"

Zechariah pointed to his mouth, and shook his head. He did his best impression of Gabriel, shaking his finger and dragging a big sword—and then he pointed at Elizabeth and mimed a woman with a big belly.

Elizabeth burst out laughing. "You are a terrible actor! Can't you just write it down?" She handed him a pad of paper from the bedside table.

Quickly, he outlined his encounter with Gabriel and passed the note to Elizabeth, who read it with disbelief.

"A baby!" she cried. "We're going to have a baby?" She fainted again, but this time, she had a smile on her face.

~

Ten months later, Elizabeth and Zechariah celebrated the birth of their new baby boy with close friends and family.

"He certainly looks like a little Zechariah!" said Joanie, Elizabeth's sister.

"He does!" said Zechariah's brother, Phil. "The spitting image. I'm gonna call him Zack."

"No, no, no," clucked Elizabeth. "His name is John."

"John?" the family questioned. "No one in our family has ever been named John. Why would you name him John?"

"You simply can't name him John, dear," said Grandma Lavinia. "My son's name is Zechariah, and his son will be named Zechariah. It's our tradition."

Elizabeth squirmed. She wished Zechariah could speak up and explain the situation. "Well, Lavinia, with all respect—Zechariah and I have both decided that his name should be John. Just ask him."

All eyes turned to Zechariah. He nodded and took up a chalkboard he had been carrying everywhere. "His name will be John, just as Elizabeth has said. It is the Lord's will," he wrote.

Instantly, Zechariah's tongue was loosened, and he could speak again! "And you, my little son, will be called the prophet of the Most High, because you will prepare the way for the Lord. You will tell His people how to find salvation through forgiveness of their sins. Because of God's tender mercy, the morning light from heaven is about to break upon us, to give light to those who sit in darkness and in the shadow of death, and to guide us to the path of peace."

God Is **Trustworthy** ～～～～～～～～～～～～

Zechariah was struck mute until his son, John, was born. He certainly learned that when God sends a message, He means it—every word!

You can depend on God to tell the truth. His word can be completely trusted, even when it seems unbelievable. Does the Bible contain some promises that you find hard to believe?

～～～～～～～～～～～～～～～～～～～～

6

God Is
a Warrior

*There is no one like the God of Israel. He rides across the
heavens to help you, across the skies in majestic splendor.
The eternal God is your refuge, and his everlasting arms
are under you. He drives out the enemy before you; he cries
out, "Destroy them!" So Israel will live in safety, prosperous
Jacob in security, in a land of grain and wine, while the
heavens drop down dew. How blessed you are, O Israel!
Who else is like you, a people saved by the LORD? He is
your protecting shield and your triumphant sword!*

DEUTERONOMY 33:26-29

You Call This an Army?

Judges 7

Gideon was a worrywart.

He urged his sons and daughters to be very cautious. It didn't pay to be too risky. Life was dangerous!

"Don't climb so high!"

"Don't run so fast!"

"Don't throw that stick!"

"Don't yell so loud!" he warned.

He knew he overdid it sometimes, but he simply couldn't help himself. The Midianites, a cruel neighboring tribe, might attack Israel at any time—and often did. So the entire Israelite community lived in constant fear, making their homes in caves, high in the hill country. They hid their gardens, harvested their wheat by moonlight, and threshed their grain in secret locations to avoid raiding parties.

One moonless night, Gideon hid himself in the bottom of a winepress to collect the grain from his wheat. As he worked feverishly to finish before dawn, an angel of the Lord interrupted him.

"God is with you, mighty warrior!" said the angel. Gideon jumped backward, tripped over some tools, and skidded across the rough wooden floor.

"Mighty? Who?" he asked.

The angel continued, "God is sending you to save Israel!"

"Me?" said Gideon, shrinking into the floorboards. "I think you've

got the wrong guy. Fighting is very dangerous, and I try to stay as safe as possible. Maybe you were looking for Gordon, my brother?"

"Quiet!" commanded the angel. "Gideon, you will lead your fellow Israelites against your enemy, the Midianites." One look at the size of that angel's sword, and Gideon decided to agree with God's messenger.

~

Gideon often had a hard time talking his own brothers into co-operating with him. And now he had to persuade an entire nation to go to war? He knew exactly how it would sound to his community. Gideon, who was afraid to fight, who lived in a cave, who threshed his wheat at night in a winepress...*that* Gideon was going to lead them in a victory against the Midianites? God would have to transform him (and his neighbors) before anyone followed him into battle!

Every morning, Gideon asked God to make him stronger and more courageous. He searched the Scriptures for wisdom and wrote down his insights and prayers in a small journal his wife made him. It took a few months, but God's Holy Spirit slowly began to reshape Gideon from the inside out.

First, Gideon felt an unnatural urge to climb the tallest oak tree he could find. Then he hiked to the top of the tallest Canaanite mountain. Finally, he found the courage to retrieve his grandfather's sword and hold the weighty piece of metal in his hands. As he turned the blade over he was overcome with a new determination to be the man God had called him to be—a warrior! With a sudden and mighty swing, Gideon turned to a watermelon sitting on the kitchen table and cut it in half, and the sword stuck fast in the wooden table underneath.

"Gideon!" cried his wife, "My table!"

Gideon smiled. He pulled the heavy sword from the wood, satisfied. No longer did he feel like a clumsy cave dweller! As God's warrior, he stood a little bit taller. After dinner he challenged his children to a footrace—and beat them for the first time.

Now he was ready to call his countrymen together!

Gideon sent word throughout the villages that all the able-bodied men should assemble in one week. God had a plan to defeat the Midianites.

~

Seven days later, Gideon surveyed his growing army, which was camped at the spring of Harod. This Israelite army of 30,000 men would make a big impression! He imagined the Israelite people someday building cities and living in real houses instead of caves. Their children would go to school without fear of a raiding party. His wife would enjoy a rooftop garden and a cistern full of clear, cold water! This army was just the beginning of good things to come.

The strong, unmistakable voice of God interrupted his daydream. "Gideon, this army is too big. Send some of the men home."

"What?" Gideon couldn't believe what he heard. "Now? They've all just arrived! Don't you see how many we have? Isn't it wonderful, God?"

"Gideon, I see things you don't. I want these people to know that I alone will win this battle," God said. "Right now, there are too many warriors. If I let this many men fight the Midianites, they will boast that they have saved themselves by their own strength. So tell them that whoever is afraid may go home."

Gideon stared at his half-chewed fingernails. What if everyone left? What if only a few thousand men stayed to fight the huge armies of the Midianites and their allies?

Despite his fears, Gideon made the announcement. Then he watched 22,000 of the men pack their belongings and head for home. With growing ulcer pains, he counted the remaining

fighting men—maybe 10,000. Surely God made a mistake!
Maybe He didn't mean to send all of those men away...Gideon
panicked and reached for his ram's horn to call them back.

"Gideon!" commanded God. "Put the horn down!"

Gideon put the horn down.

"Why are you frightened? Who's in charge here? You or Me?"

"You, Lord," said Gideon.

"That's right, and there are still too many men here," God said.

Gideon started to protest but was shushed. "Do what I
say," God said. "Take all the remaining men down
to the river, tell them to take a drink, and watch
them carefully. Put those who cup the water in their
hands in one group, and put those who lap the
water directly out of the river in another group."

Lapper-Uppers? Water Cuppers? Gideon pinched the bridge of
his nose. He had a headache. He wished he had more than ten
fingernails to chew. Still, he did not hesitate, but gave the command:
"Everyone down to the river for a mandatory drink!" Most of the
men rolled their eyes when they heard what Gideon wanted them
to do. Nevertheless, they all knelt down and tasted the water.
Immediately, they were separated into the two groups—the
Water Cuppers and the Lapper-Uppers.

God spoke to Gideon again. "All right. I've seen enough. I will win
this war with just the Water Cuppers. Tell the others that they are
excused."

"Excused?" exclaimed Gideon. "Sent home? Lord, You must have counted wrong! You mean the Lapper-Uppers, don't You? O God, look at the difference in numbers! Why, there are only—"

"Three hundred Water Cuppers," God said, "and that's all I need. With these three hundred, I'll rescue the people and give victory to the Israelites. Now meet Me in your tent to hear the rest of My plan."

Flummoxed and a bit weary, Gideon sent the surprised Lapper-Uppers home before retreating to his tent. He wasn't sure what to expect anymore—only that it would be incredible.

He was right! God's plan would surprise even the most seasoned soldier.

~

That night, Gideon woke the Israelite camp at 11:45. "Everybody up! Now is the time!"

He split the men into three divisions and directed the weapons supply team to assign each soldier a ram's horn, a clay pot, and a torch.

The men were understandably irritated. "First you whittle our numbers down to nothing, and then you give us cooking tools and a trumpet? We came to fight a battle! Where are our swords?"

Gideon paced back and forth in front of the troops. He listened to all their complaints and nodded. "I know! I understand! But these are God's weapons. Let's just do as He says and watch Him fight for us," replied

Gideon. "He will not disappoint us. His ways will amaze you and scare the pants off your enemies!"

Bolstered by Gideon's confident leadership, the Israelite army tucked their clay pots under their arms and silently crept to the edge of the Midianite camp.

After the changing of the guard, Gideon whistled. The first division of troops blew their horns as loudly as possible and smashed their clay pots with a crash. The second and third divisions immediately followed suit. Then, the 300 men lit their torches and shouted together, "A sword for the Lord and for Gideon!"

Terrified, the Midianites jumped out of their beds, plowed through their barracks, and collided with one another in total panic. They held their ears with both hands, trying to shut out the blast of the ram horns, and ran aimlessly into the darkness in their nightshirts, abandoning their weapons, their clothing, and their camp.

The Israelites watched their enemies flee into the night with awe. Only God could cause such confusion and fear with kitchen utensils!

What a stunning God we serve! thought Gideon.

He was once an intimidated man hiding in a winepress, but now, Gideon had the privilege of being God's mighty warrior, leading the Israelites in a victory only He could provide.

God Is a Warrior

God is the ultimate warrior. All the brains and brawn in the world can't compare to Mighty God! He does the impossible every time.

The Bible is full of God's victories. Want more? Check out 1 Samuel 14, where young Prince Jonathan and his armor bearer bravely set out against a Philistine outpost—all by themselves! They too understood that with God on their side, nothing is too big or impossible.

Are you in the middle of a battle? Call on God for backup. His plans are foolproof.

7

God Is

Incomparable & Almighty

Who else has held the oceans in his hand? Who has measured off the heavens with his fingers? Who else knows the weight of the earth or has weighed out the mountains and the hills on a scale? Who is able to advise the Spirit of the Lord?... All the nations of the world are but a drop in the bucket. They are nothing more than dust on the scales. He picks up the whole earth as though it were a grain of sand... "To whom will you compare me? Who is my equal?" asks the Holy One.

ISAIAH 40:12-13,15,25

I am the LORD, and there is no other. I create the light and make the darkness. I send good times and bad times. I, the LORD, am the one who does these things.

ISAIAH 45:6-7

Take That, Baal!

1 Kings 18–19

They didn't call King Ahab "wicked" for nothing!

He did more evil in the sight of the Lord than any other ruler before him. You name it, he did it: idol worship, infant sacrifice, lying, adultery, and much, much more. He had a blatant disregard for God's law and a hard heart. King Ahab refused to repent.

"That's enough!" God said. He called on his prophet Elijah to give King Ahab a message. "Elijah, give Mr. Know-It-All notice: Thanks to all his wickedness, there will be a great drought in the land. There will be no rain, no dew…no moisture whatsoever until I say the word."

Three long, waterless years passed before God gave Elijah a new message for King Ahab. Following God's orders, Elijah returned to the palace to speak with the king.

"You!" screamed Ahab when he saw Elijah. "The troublemaker comes again! Where have you been hiding?"

"Me?" replied Elijah in mock surprise. "I didn't cause any trouble! I just brought you the bad news. You are the troublemaker! Tired of the drought yet?"

King Ahab drew his sword, "I should kill you right now!"

"That seems unsportsman-like," said Elijah. "Why don't we have a contest instead?"

"A contest? Like what?"

Elijah stepped closer. "How about this, King Ahab. Invite all of Israel to Mount Carmel. Bring the four hundred fifty prophets of your pretend god Baal and the four hundred prophets of your made-up god Asherah. I'll show up with the incomparable Almighty God of Israel. Then we'll see whose God is real—unless, of course, you don't really think Baal and Asherah are worthy adversaries for God Almighty."

King Ahab hated to be challenged. He hated Elijah even more. "You're on!" he shouted.

~

The bright blue, cloudless sky made a dramatic backdrop for the battle between the prophets. The entire population of Israel gathered on Mt. Carmel, surrounding Elijah and the 850 pagan prophets, who were busy strategizing their game plan for the day.

Elijah signaled for the crowd's attention.

"People of Israel! It's time to get off the fence! Either choose to follow Baal or choose to follow the Lord of lords, the commander of the heavenly hosts, and our nation's ultimate leader, Almighty God!"

The people were silent. Elijah continued.

"This is what will happen today. The prophets of Baal and I will stack firewood on an altar and slaughter an ox on top. But neither of us will set fire to the wood underneath. The prophets of Baal will pray to Baal, and I will pray to the Lord, and the one who answers by setting fire to the wood will prove to be the true God."

Everyone cheered and applauded. This sounded like a good show!

"And because I'm such a nice guy," finished Elijah, "I'd like to invite the prophets of Baal to go first. Just remember, no matches!"

The prophets of Baal went into action. They slaughtered their ox, cut it apart, and arranged the pieces on top of their altar. Then they began praying and chanting to Baal in earnest. They went on and on...but nothing happened. So they
yelled louder! And danced!

Hours passed. Not even a whisper of a breeze touched the air. Around noon, Elijah couldn't keep quiet any longer.

"Hey guys, you've got to shout louder! Maybe Baal is in the bathroom or deep in thought somewhere. Wait, wait...I know! He's on vacation! Or asleep? That's it—he can't hear you! Wake him up!"

The prophets of Baal responded by going bananas. They cut themselves with knives and swords and screamed until they were hoarse. After two more hours of their nonsense, Elijah stepped in.

"Okay, enough of this! Now it's my turn. Everybody gather around."

Elijah gathered 12 big stones, which represented the 12 tribes of Israel, and repaired his altar, which the prophets of Baal had torn down. Then he dug a wide trench around the big flat-topped rock and filled the trench with water until it overflowed. Finally, Elijah poured more water over the ox, the wood, and the rocks until everything was wet through and through. Then Elijah prayed.

"O holy God, let these people know right now that You alone are incomparable and almighty and that Your rule is supreme! I am Your servant, and I am doing only as You have instructed me to do. So please, Lord, answer me and show these people that You are giving them a chance to ask for forgiveness and return to You today."

Instantly, blazing fire from heaven engulfed Elijah's altar. The ox and wood were reduced to ash, and the intense heat licked up every drop of moisture from the trench. Nothing but a blackened crater remained.

"Almighty God!" screamed the Israelites, flattening

themselves to the ground. "God Almighty rules! He is the one true God!"

King Ahab's mouth fell open, his eyebrows shot up, and eyes opened wide. He couldn't stop staring at the smoking ash heap.

"King Ahab!" shouted Elijah. "How do you like that? Is there any question whose God rules now?"

King Ahab walked silently to the crater and bent to inspect the charred ground. He ran his hand through the scorched dirt, speechless. Then he stood up, turned around, and fired all 850 prophets of Baal on the spot.

"Go and prepare a nice meal for yourself, King Ahab," said Elijah. "I hear there is a fierce rainstorm coming!"

That evening the rains began, bringing healing to the parched land. No one doubted God's supremacy any longer. He proved Himself incomparable and almighty.

God Is Incomparable & Almighty

King Ahab and his wife, Jezebel, believed in fake gods, such as Asherah and Baal. But those gods were only man-made statues without any power. The Almighty God is completely different. There is only one of Him! He created the heavens and the earth and set life into motion. And He watches over His creation every day.

We may think we don't have false gods, or idols, but we actually do! They are the things that we think are more important than God. They can come in all shapes and sizes. Whom or what do you put first in your life?

8

God
Refreshes

*Come to me, all of you who are weary and carry heavy
burdens, and I will give you rest. Take my yoke upon
you. Let me teach you, because I am humble and gentle
at heart, and you will find rest for your souls. For my
yoke is easy to bear, and the burden I give you is light.*

MATTHEW 11:28-30

*Blessed are those who trust in the LORD and have made
the LORD their hope and confidence. They are like trees
planted along a riverbank, with roots that reach deep
into the water. Such trees are not bothered by the heat
or worried by long months of drought. Their leaves stay
green, and they go right on producing delicious fruit.*

JEREMIAH 17:7-8

*Those who trust in the LORD will find new strength.
They will soar high on wings like eagles. They will run
and not grow weary. They will walk and not faint.*

ISAIAH 40:31

Even Victories Are Tiring
1 Kings 18–19

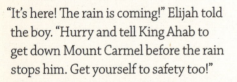

A small cloud, barely big enough to notice, dotted the sky far out to sea. It looked like nothing much, but the prophet Elijah had instructed the boy to tell him about any speck on the horizon. So the boy ran back up the hill and reported the small dark cloud.

"It's here! The rain is coming!" Elijah told the boy. "Hurry and tell King Ahab to get down Mount Carmel before the rain stops him. Get yourself to safety too!"

Elijah had just won a major battle—a test between wicked King Ahab's prophets of Baal and himself, prophet of the one true God Almighty. The coming rainstorm was a sign of God's rule, ending a three-year drought that had turned the country into a parched and cracked wasteland.

The boy had barely spoken the words of warning to King Ahab when the first clap of thunder shook the air. Rattled, King Ahab abandoned the meal he was eating and jumped into his chariot. He whipped his horses into a frenzy, taking off in a cloud of dust.

King Ahab's chariot hurtled over the rough path toward the city of Jezreel moments ahead of the dark clouds and rain. He held the reins in his right hand and braced himself against the side of the chariot with his left, racing along the edge of the fierce storm. Raindrops as big as marbles splattered against his face. He blinked wildly to clear his eyes from the downpour.

All at once, King Ahab pulled up on the reins. Elijah had darted out in front of the royal chariot, charging straight down the mountain! Within a few moments, he pulled ahead, easily outpacing King Ahab.

Elijah's breathing was easy, his legs were loose, and he didn't feel even a twinge of fatigue—God had infused him with supernatural strength and renewed energy.

Things will be different after today, thought Elijah. *Ahab has seen the work of the Almighty God, and so have the people. No one can deny God's power now!*

Elijah never slowed his pace or stopped for a breather until he arrived at the gates of the king's palace in Jezreel. He rested in the courtyard until King Ahab rushed inside the palace to tell his wife, Jezebel, the latest news.

"Well? What happened?" Queen Jezebel asked. "Did you kill that pesky Elijah?"

"Not exactly," replied King Ahab.

"Not exactly? Wasn't that the point? The odds were eight hundred fifty to one!"

"Well, he won the contest," said King Ahab, shaking his head. "You should have seen it, Jezebel! It was unbelievable. You know what happened? His God sent fire down from heaven that burned his sacrifice to ashes. Ashes! It even consumed the altar rocks—nothing left but cinders! It was crazy," the king exclaimed.

Jezebel shook with anger. "You mean to tell me you didn't kill him? Elijah is still alive?"

"Like I said, you should have been there, Jezebel!"

"So what happened to my prophets? Where are they now?"

"Well, uh…it's like…" stumbled King Ahab. "I had to fire them. For good."

Queen Jezebel's face flushed a deep red, and her mouth began to twitch. "Are you saying what I think you are saying? Are my prophets dead?" Queen Jezebel's voice grew louder with each word. Then she shouted, "You were supposed to kill Elijah, not my prophets!"

"Now, honey, calm down," hushed the king. "You're getting too excited. And you know what happens when you get excited. You do rash things that you regret the next morning."

Jezebel drove a finger deep into Ahab's chest until he was walking backward. "Oh, dear husband," she snarled, "I will not regret anything in the morning."

~

That evening a courier delivered a note to Elijah in the palace courtyard.

Dearest Elijah,

You are a dead man.
Enjoy your last night on earth!

Love,
Jezebel

Elijah slowly refolded the note and tucked it into his cloak. He said "thank you" to the courier, tipped him a few coins, and strolled toward the palace gates.

Elijah casually meandered outside the courtyard, hoping the palace attendants thought he was on his way to dinner. He waved and gave them two thumbs-up, pretending that everything was just fine. But as soon as Elijah was out of sight, he began running. He picked up speed outside the city gates until he was sprinting down the highway toward Beersheba, a city far south in Judah.

Ninety-two miles later, Elijah collapsed in the shade of a small broom tree and hung his head between his knees. His chest was heaving, and his side ached as he tried to catch his breath. Then he began to cry. He was exhausted.

"God," sobbed Elijah, "where are You now? I thought we just had a victory—but come on! Now Jezebel wants *me* dead too." He hiccuped. "When does it all stop? I'm tired, I'm hungry, and my feet hurt. You know how many miles I've just run? I'd rather be dead!"

Elijah rolled to the ground dramatically and screamed toward the sky. "Take me out of my misery!"

Elijah cried until he couldn't make another tear. Then with a stuffy nose and bloodshot eyes, he rolled over on his side and fell fast asleep in the dirt.

Minutes? Hours? Days? He didn't know how long he'd lain there when an angel of the Lord shook him awake. "Hey...come on, wake up. You need to eat."

Elijah cracked one eye open and found a loaf of fresh bread and a jug of water next to his head. He slowly propped himself up on one elbow, stuffed the bread in his mouth, and drank the water. Then he lay down again and began to snore.

The angel of God came back a second time and shook Elijah.

"Elijah...wake up. I've brought more bread and water. This is supernatural food, so eat up! Drink! It will give you the energy you need to get where you're going. You have an appointment with God, and you don't want to be late. You've got questions and He's got answers. You say you're ready to give up, but there's more to this story than you understand."

Wearily, Elijah sat up and followed the angel's directions. He ate every scrap of God's bread, licked every crumb from his fingers, and drank the entire jug of water. Then he took a deep breath. He really didn't want to go anywhere, but the angel had said there was more to know. And God wanted to talk to him. So Elijah pulled himself upright and stretched.

No muscle aches? No stiffness?

He gingerly reached for his toes. No pain at all! As a matter of fact, Elijah had never felt so refreshed in his life. He cut down a walking stick from the broom tree and set off down the road, shading his eyes from the bright sun. He had a long way to go, but now he looked forward to the journey. God wasn't finished with him yet.

God Refreshes

Elijah was physically exhausted, afraid for his life, and outrageously hungry. Have you ever felt completely drained? Maybe you haven't run four marathons in a row or had your life threatened by a queen, but that doesn't mean you haven't felt wiped out! Everybody gets tired. That's when it's time for some food from God.

God promises new strength to those who trust in Him. All we have to do is hand over our burdens to our extra-strong God. He longs to restore our souls. Got troubles? Try talking with God about them. He will refresh you.

(To find out what happened to Elijah, read 1 Kings 19.)

9

God Is
Worthy of Awe

Why do you not tremble in my presence? I, the LORD, define the ocean's sandy shoreline as an everlasting boundary that the waters cannot cross. The waves may toss and roar, but they can never pass the boundaries I set.

JEREMIAH 5:22

The Fiery Furnace
Daniel 3

After conquering Jerusalem, King Nebuchadnezzar of Babylon sent many of the young Hebrew captives to a special Babylonian school for training in his royal service. One young Hebrew named Daniel proved quite impressive. He had a God-given gift of deciphering dreams and visions.

Thanks to this gift of wisdom, Daniel rose through the Babylonian administration, quickly earning a position at the king's court. With his newfound advantages, Daniel requested that his friends Shadrach, Meshach, and Abednego (also Hebrews) be appointed new jobs as well. Because of Daniel's recommendation, these three were put in charge of the province of Babylon.

Shadrach, Meshach, and Abednego excelled in their new employment. Under their leadership, the province of Babylon flourished. King Nebuchadnezzar couldn't have been more pleased. With economic policies succeeding on the home front, he really had something to brag about to the neighboring Aramaeans.

In a show of grandeur, King Nebuchadnezzar commissioned a 90-foot tall gold statue of his god and namesake, Nabu, to be built on the plain of Dura. King Nebuchadnezzar was very proud of his statue.

"Have you seen the ninety-foot version of me?" he bragged.

"Impressive, eh? It's so big the Aramaeans can see it from their kitchen windows!"

Two months after the completion of the statue, the surrounding gardens began to bloom. The imported myrtle trees glistened with morning dew, and the date palms and pomegranate trees bowed with ripened fruit. A stone pathway that led to the base of the golden statue was inscribed with the words, "I am Nebuchadnezzar, king of Babylon, who made this." King Nebuchadnezzar pointed out the words to anyone who could read.

Invitations to the dedication ceremony were mailed to every politician and dignitary in the region. The festivities would include juggling monkeys, talking parrots, elephants on roller skates balancing on small balls...no one would forget this party! Strict rules for the occasion were also included in the invitation.

Officials! When the band begins to play, fall down on your faces and worship the great Nabu, god of Nebuchadnezzar! Full and immediate cooperation is demanded. Those who don't obey will be thrown into a blazing furnace.

P.S. Please refrain from feeding the monkeys. If you get too close, they will throw poop.

Immediately after receiving their invites, Shadrach, Meshach, and Abednego met together to discuss the party instructions.

"Of all the things to be asked to do!" complained Meshach. "And he comes up with worshipping a statue?"

"What did you expect?" asked Abednego.

"But it's a statue!" said Meshach. "A big hunk of metal! Why would anyone worship that?"

"I know," said Shadrach. "It's ridiculous. We can't bow before a false god—not today, not tomorrow...not ever!"

He put his fist into the center of their small circle. "Are you with me, guys? To the furnace!"

The other two put their hands on top of his. "To the furnace," they said, disheartened.

~

Two weeks later a circus-like atmosphere surrounded the statue of Nabu. Elephants adorned with red ribbons and body paint roller-skated through the lush gardens. Monkeys juggled fruit in the treetops, and the emerald green and yellow parrots told party guests riddles and funny jokes.

"What happened when the man stole the pig? It squealed to the police!"

"What is brown and sticky? A stick!"

"What's orange and sounds like a parrot? A carrot!"

Around three in the afternoon, trumpeting heralds announced that the time had come to worship Nabu.

Shadrach, Meshach, and Abednego hung near the rear of the procession, hoping to avoid attention. However, when the band began to play the national anthem and everyone but the three young Hebrew men bowed to the golden statue, they stood out. Literally.

~

That evening, King Nebuchadnezzar asked for a full account of the party.

"Everything went perfectly!" reported a palace envoy. "The statue was polished and gleaming, the gardens dripped with flowers...oh, and the food! It was a really great party. Well, except..."

"Except for what?" asked King Nebuchadnezzar.

"Except for the three Hebrews who refused to bow down to your golden statue—Meshach, Shadrach, and Abednego, the governors of the Babylon province."

"Daniel's friends?" asked King Nebuchadnezzar. "That's surprising! I thought the invitations were very straightforward. Let's have a talk with them. Bring them here immediately!"

At the king's request, the three men were quickly assembled before him.

"There must have been a misunderstanding," began King

Nebuchadnezzar. "I heard today that the three of you refused to bow down to my golden statue. Maybe you didn't understand the directions. When you hear the national anthem, you bow down to Nabu. Now, I'm very willing to give you another chance because I'd hate to lose three of my best governors."

Shadrach stepped forward to speak for the group.

"King Nebuchadnezzar, we are very thankful for our privileged employment. Working for you has been very pleasant! However, we cannot bow down to any idol, even one made in your honor. We understand this might mean our deaths, but our God is perfectly able to deliver us from a fiery furnace or any other punishment. I'm sorry, King, we cannot bow to your golden statue."

King Nebuchadnezzar's nostrils flared!

"How impetuous! How ridiculous! Don't you realize I'm the king—and your boss? I rule all of Babylon! You will either do what I say or die."

"I'm sorry, King, we cannot bow to your golden statue," repeated Shadrach.

King Nebuchadnezzar banged his fists against the armrests of his marble throne. "Fine! You've made your own decision. Guards!"

Three guards gripped the Hebrew men and hurried them down the gilded hall.

King Nebuchadnezzar called out the door, "Heat the furnace seven times hotter than usual! As hot as it will go! Make it sizzle! I want those lippy, ill-mannered oafs tied up and thrown in the oven like barbecued beef!"

Down at the furnace, workers stoked the fire until it could get no hotter. Shadrach, Meshach, and Abednego were bound with ropes, hoisted into the air, and pitched through the opening of the furnace.

The scalding heat immediately began to blister their skin—

but just on the other side of the furnace doors, the intensity melted into a cool, refreshing balm. Fire raged all around them, but it did not harm them. Shadrach, Meshach, and Abednego wriggled out of their ropes and looked at each other, astonished.

King Nebuchadnezzar had come to the furnace to witness their execution. When they seemed to be unhurt, he jumped to his feet and began pointing excitedly.

"Why aren't they dead? And didn't we just throw three men into that fire? Who is that other man—he looks like a son of the gods! What kind of magic is this?" The king didn't wait for answers, but called out, "Meshach! Shadrach! Abednego! Return to me immediately!"

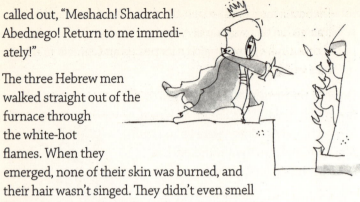

The three Hebrew men walked straight out of the furnace through the white-hot flames. When they emerged, none of their skin was burned, and their hair wasn't singed. They didn't even smell like smoke!

Many of the Babylonian witnesses shrank back in alarm, but King Nebuchadnezzar came forward, touched the men with reverence, and realized that he had just seen a miracle.

"Blessed be your God, who has rescued you! Even in the face of my wrath, your faith did not waver. Therefore, I hereby issue a new decree: Anyone who says a bad word about the God of Meshach, Shadrach, and Abednego will be killed immediately—limbs torn apart and homes burned down. There has never been another God who could do something like this!"

The three friends hugged one another and praised the Lord.

"Oh, and one more thing," said the king. "I take back what I said about barbecue beef. Promotions for all of you!"

God Is Worthy of Awe

These days, we call everything from new shoes to video games "awesome." In reality, when something is awesome, it inspires reverence and wonder. God should inspire both of those responses in us every day. He is more worthy of true awe than anyone or anything.

The adventures of Shadrach, Meshach, Abednego, and Daniel don't stop at the fiery furnace. The book of Daniel is chock-full of awe-inspiring stories about God. Let Him take your breath away!

〜〜〜〜〜〜〜〜〜〜〜〜〜〜〜〜〜〜〜〜〜〜〜

10

God Is

Timeless, Ageless, & Eternal

*Listen to me, O family of Jacob, Israel my chosen
one! I alone am God, the First and the Last. It was
my hand that laid the foundations of the earth, my
right hand that spread out the heavens above. When
I call out the stars, they all appear in order.*

Isaiah 48:12-13

*In the beginning, Lord, you laid the foundation of the earth
and made the heavens with your hands. They will perish,
but you remain forever. They will wear out like old clothing.
You will fold them up like a cloak and discard them like old
clothing. But you are always the same; you will live forever.*

Hebrews 1:10-12

God Loves Old People Too

Genesis 15-18

God gave Abram a message on his seventy-fifth birthday.

"Abram! Leave your native country, your relatives, and your father's family, and go to the land that I will show you. I will make you into a great nation. I will bless you and make you famous, and you will be a blessing to others. I will bless those who bless you and curse those who curse you. All the families on earth will be blessed through you."

"Wow," said Abram, "that's big!"

When he told his wife, Sarai, about God's message, she had a lot of questions he wished he'd thought to ask.

"How long will we be gone, Abram? A few months? Years? Will we ever return?"

"I don't know," said Abram. "We've just got to trust God."

"But how many plates should I pack? All of them? What about our fine china? Sheets, blankets, books? Golf clubs? Swimsuits? And you said I'm going to be a mother—can you give me a little more information? I'm not getting any younger, you know."

Abram reluctantly shrugged his shoulders.

"I really don't know, dear. God will reveal His plan along the way."

So Sarai packed their everyday dishes as well as the fine china. She divided their winter and summer clothes into separate suitcases and labeled them with big letters. If they were going to be gone a long time (maybe forever), she certainly wanted to know where her warm sweaters were when it got cold.

The next Sunday, Abram and Sarai unpegged their tent and began traveling in the direction God pointed. They didn't look back.

~

Years passed. Everywhere Abram went, God protected him and made room for him in the land. Abram and Sarai prospered as God's promises came true. But there was still one part of the covenant that bothered Abram. God had promised he would be a father to a whole nation. Sarai still hadn't gotten pregnant, and he was a much older old man now, so naturally he wondered how he could become a father without children.

One evening as dusk settled into night, Abram went outside and shook his fist at the sky.

"God! I know You haven't forgotten me. I've been blessed with big harvests, livestock, and a brand new top-of-the-line tent. But You also promised me a nation. You said I would be a father! So how can I be the father of a nation when I don't have kids? What good is all this wealth? One of my servants will end up with everything You've given me."

The Lord heard Abram's complaint and responded. "Abram, Abram, Abram. Who do you think I am? I don't promise things and then go back on My word! A servant is not going to inherit your wealth. You are going to have a son of your own. Now, look up into the sky."

Abram craned his neck backward. All he saw was a big, black universe lit with tiny lights.

one . two . three
four . five . six ...

"What do you see?" asked God.

"A big black void. Endless space."

"What about those stars?" God asked. "Can you count them? Let's see you try."

Abram began ticking off the tiny lights but quickly lost his place.

"Too many?" God laughed. "Well, that's a picture of your descendants, Abram— too many to count."

Too many to count. A family as numerous as the stars!

Abram believed God, and in return, God declared him righteous because of his faith.

~

Even more years passed—many more.

Sarai cut Abram's chocolate birthday cake into generous pieces and passed them out to his friends and family. It was Abram's ninety-ninth birthday!

He smiled as his party guests complimented him on such a long, prosperous life. He thanked his friends for their generous gifts. Another goat! Fourteen dozen eggs! A new walking stick and a light blue wool coat!

Smile, smile, smile.

Finally, three hours later, Abram collapsed into his recliner. The guests had gone home, and another birthday had passed. He ran a hand over his balding head and rubbed his eyes. Sarai handed him a glass of warm milk.

"Abram," she said. "You look worn out. Didn't you have a good birthday? Too much cake? What's wrong?"

"I'm only tired," said Abram. He didn't want to talk about what was really on his mind. *Didn't God promise me a son…twice?* He sipped his milk. *When will God fulfill His promise? Will God ever fulfill His promise?*

Sarai covered Abram with a curly-haired ramskin throw. "Rest here," she said. "I'll clean up."

Abram admired her as he watched her leave. She still looked beautiful—specially for an 89-year-old! He finished his milk and closed his eyes. Maybe they'd have a son next year.

"Didn't think I'd show up for your ninety-ninth birthday?"

Startled, Abram jumped alert. "God?"

"I didn't forget you," said God. "In fact, I'm here to renew the promise I made you and to give you a new gift."

Abraham threw the ramskin blanket to the ground and scrambled to his feet. God was at his home talking to him!

"From now on, you'll have a new name—Abraham, father of many nations. I will be your God, and you and your descendants will be My people. I'm giving your wife a new name too. From now on she will be called Sarah. And she *is* going to have a baby."

Abraham fell on his face before God. He stretched out his arms in prayerful worship and thanks. Then he got up, ran to Sarah, and started twirling her around the kitchen.

"O great Almighty God! You are so good to me! Thank You—*woo hoo hoo!*" Happy laughter spilled into his prayer. "You (*ha ha ha!*) are making me (*wah ha hooey!*), a ninety-nine-year-old man (*whoa ho ho!*), a father?" Tears of joy rolled down both his cheeks.

"That's right," confirmed God. "This time next year, Sarah is going to have a son. My timing is always perfect."

Abraham wiped the tears from his face with the back of his sleeve and tried to catch his breath, but he couldn't stop smiling. Birthdays, he knew, would never be the same.

God Is Timeless, Ageless, & Eternal

Abram waited 25 years for God's promise to be fulfilled. He thought it was an awfully long time to wait, but God didn't see it that way. God holds all of eternity in His hands, and He isn't affected by time. He doesn't grow older as minutes tick by. He is not impressed with the changing fashions. He is the same yesterday, today, and forever!

That's why you can count on God's Word to remain true whether you read it today or in ten years. Our world may change, but our God never does.

Has God promised you something? Don't doubt that He'll fulfill his promises—He will! But He will do it in His timing, not yours.

11

God Is

Sufficient for All Your Needs

What is impossible for people is possible with God.

Luke 18:27

The Rich Man
Luke 18:18-27

Davis rode a pedigreed camel named Pomegranate Twist. His was not only the best-looking camel in town but also the best dressed. Davis's bridle and saddle were embroidered with imported silk threads to match the custom suits he wore to work at the temple.

His wardrobe was full of fine clothing and shoes. Davis kept his Italian-leather sandals oiled and looking good and made time to visit a salon twice a week. He wouldn't dream of being seen without a fresh manicure and his eyebrows waxed. He also never left home with less than 65 gold pieces in his satchel. Who knew what the day might hold? He wanted to be ready for anything.

Davis had inherited most of his wealth from his father, a successful textile merchant who had built a thriving trade with the Phoenicians. Rather than take over the family business, Davis dabbled in the cloth trade as a hobby, having chosen a career as a church leader at the local synagogue instead. He spent his days studying Scripture and memorizing verses to teach to the congregation. Davis had a very satisfying life—a fulfilling career, lots of money, good friends, and a well-developed prayer routine. Things really couldn't get much better.

One day, Jesus came to town. Immediately, the ruler of the local synagogue organized a special meeting so leaders and parishioners could ask questions of Jesus, the wisest teacher their faith had ever known. People in the synagogue began making lists of questions to ask Jesus, and Davis was no exception. He agonized over what to ask. He wanted to appear sophisticated...but not too highbrow. Jesus was a man of the people. After many hours of research at his home office and a garbage can overflowing with crumpled-up queries, he settled on one simple but profound question: What must a person do to attain eternal life? Satisfied, Davis put down his quill, turned out the light, and went to bed.

~

The night of the meet and greet, Jesus was seated at the front of the synagogue, facing the congregation. The religious teachers lined up with their notecards and waited patiently as Jesus took time to answer each question.

Finally, after what felt like forever, Davis reached the front of the line. He was surprised at how unremarkable Jesus looked up close. He certainly hadn't dressed up for the interviews, that much was clear. His nails had not been polished. His beard was a little... scruffy. However, Jesus commanded respect. His eyes transfixed His listeners with their intensity.

Davis smoothed down the collar of his dinner jacket and stepped forward.

"Rabbi Jesus," he said with a formal bow, "how nice to meet You. I've heard such wonderful things about Your teachings. We are blessed to have this opportunity to bring You these questions today."

Jesus smiled. "It's great to meet you too, Davis."

 Davis stared blankly at Jesus, plainly startled. *How did He know my name? Did I introduce myself?*

"Well, good Teacher," recovered Davis, "there are many mysteries about God—so many questions to ask as we study the Scriptures. However, I think this one question sums them all up. What must I do to get eternal life?"

Jesus didn't answer right away. Instead, He thoughtfully examined Davis.

It wasn't long before Davis began to fidget. Those eyes! He's looking right into my soul! Did I ask a dumb question? Do I have food on my face? Is my lapel folded incorrectly?

"So, good Teacher..." Davis said, nervously breaking the silence.

Jesus put a hand up. "Why do you call Me good? Only God is truly good, you know."

Davis blushed. "I...I meant..."

"It's okay," said Jesus, a twinkle in His eye. "Your question is a good one. How does one get eternal life? Well, you know the commandments." Jesus ticked them off on his fingertips. "Do not commit adultery, do not murder, do not steal, do not lie, honor your mother and father."

Davis sighed, relaxing his shoulders. "Thank goodness—I've kept all those. I have made it my life's work to obey the law of Moses."

"Ah," replied Jesus, "that's good! But there is one thing you haven't done, Davis. Sell everything you have and give the money to the poor. Then come follow Me. I can use a good teacher like you."

Jesus's words hung heavy in the temple air. Davis twitched uncomfortably in the silence. He didn't know how to answer! *Jesus probably doesn't understand who I am. To sell everything I have... um, that would be...well, a lot! Certainly, Jesus couldn't mean everything.* "Sell everything?"

"Everything."

"Everything?" Davis questioned again. "I have many things. Which do you mean? My clothes? My home? My camel?"

"Sell all of it. Then come work with Me."

"What about my textile trade?"

"It's only a hobby. Let it go."

"But what about my investments? I just remodeled my beach home. I bought three purebred Arabian mares. I'm privately labeling my own olive oil!" Davis twisted the end of his dinner jacket as if he were wringing water from a washcloth. "Maybe I could use the proceeds of my new investments for the advancement of the poor?"

"Sell everything but the sandals on your feet," Jesus said. "Then come follow Me."

Davis's tanned face lost all its color. Beads of sweat lined his upper lip and temples. He squirmed. He twitched. A sudden fever flared through his body. *Leave everything? All my possessions? Be left with nothing?* He just...couldn't. He wouldn't! Though his heart felt as if it were ripping in half, Davis turned and hurried away without so much as a goodbye.

"How hard it is for rich people to get into the kingdom of God!" Jesus explained when Davis had left the sanctuary. "It's easier for a camel to go through the eye of a needle than for a rich person to enter the kingdom of God!"

Davis's coworkers watched this exchange with trembling. "Then who in the world can be saved?" they whispered.

Jesus heard their mumbling and addressed the whole crowd. "What is impossible for people is possible with God."

Meanwhile, back at his home, Davis kicked off his sandals at the front door and ran up the spiral staircase, taking two steps at a time. He dove for his bed and slipped between his silk sheets, heartsick. He hurt inside. On one hand, he had everything a man could want. But on the other hand, he felt empty inside. Jesus's words echoed in his mind. *Come and follow Me.*

God Is **Sufficient for All Your Needs**

Davis, the rich man, had a heart problem. He felt secure because he was wealthy, not because he trusted God to take care of him. Jesus wasn't telling him to get rid of his money because it was bad to be rich—Jesus was pointing out that as long as he relied on his own ability to succeed, he would be missing out on something better. God alone is able to meet all our needs.

Everybody would like a little more of this and that! However, we must be extra careful about letting *things* rule our hearts. If money and possessions come before God, we've got a heart problem, and living out a godly life is going to be as hard as shoving a camel through an itty-bitty hole in a needle.

Don't rely on yourself, your own schemes, or your own money. Rely on God. He is all you need.

12

God Is
Knowable

Don't let the wise boast in their wisdom, or the powerful boast in their power, or the rich boast in their riches. But those who wish to boast should boast in this alone: that they truly know me and understand that I am the LORD who demonstrates unfailing love and who brings justice and righteousness to the earth, and that I delight in these things. I, the LORD, have spoken!

JEREMIAH 9:23-24

Let's Have a Party!

Luke 10:38-42

Mary! Mary?" Martha stood at her back door and hollered through the orange grove. "Where are you?"

Mary didn't answer. Flustered, Martha gathered her skirts and marched into the orchard, pushing back the fruit-laden branches as she made her way down the rows. At the far end of the orange grove she found her sister curled up on a small wooden bench, reading poetry.

"Mary! It's two o'clock!"

Mary marked her place with a finger and looked up at her older sister. "Already?"

"Yes, already! And you haven't milked the goat! Or started the bread! What will we do without bread, Mary? This is a party! For Jesus!"

"Calm down, Martha." Mary stood up and brushed a few stray leaves off her dress. "Everything will be perfect. Your parties always are! You are the ultimate hostess."

"Well, it can't be perfect if we don't have bread or milk! So are you coming? Everyone will be here by six."

"Yes, of course," replied Mary, rolling up her scroll of poetry. "You just wait until you taste my bread. You're going to faint, it'll be so good."

Martha rolled her eyes. "Really." She was not amused by her little sister's easygoing attitude. "We'll see about that. There are about a million things to do besides make bread and strain the milk..." She began rattling off the items on her growing to-do list as the two made their way back to the house.

Martha felt as if six o'clock came much too quickly! The guests began arriving earlier than planned, sending her into a frenzy of activity. She scurried about the house, fluffing pillows and refilling glasses with her signature strawberry lemonade.

"Ice? Napkins? Anything else?" she questioned the disciples. "Would you like an appetizer? Melon bites or a fig tart?" But she ran around the room so quickly, pouring drinks and offering snacks, that the guests didn't even have time to answer.

Meanwhile, Mary pulled the loaves of bread from the oven and set them on racks to cool while mentally ticking through Martha's to-do list: set the table, chill the milk, fill the party pitcher, garnish the lamb stew with mint leaves…Yep, everything was ready! She untied her apron, folded it on a kitchen chair, and took a cold glass of water into the living room, where the rest of the guests relaxed. With a contented sigh, she sat down on the floor next to Jesus, who was telling one of her favorite stories—the parable of the good Samaritan.

"Then a priest came down the road," Jesus said. "He saw the poor, suffering man lying in the ditch, but he passed by on the other side of the road." The disciples and Mary shook their heads. "Not long after," Jesus continued, "another man walked down the road, this time a Samar—"

"Mary? Where are you? Mary!" Martha's hand clasped her sister's shoulder, interrupting Jesus's story. "There you are!" She looked at their guests. "Please excuse us!" Pulling on Mary's sleeve, Martha whispered fiercely into her ear. "It's time to set the table!"

"I already did it," replied Mary.

"But you didn't fill the butter dish!" Martha said. "And the bread has cooled now, so you can slice it."

"Couldn't I do that in just a moment?" asked Mary. "Jesus was right in the middle of a story."

Martha threw her hands in the air and looked imploringly at Jesus. "Don't You care that my sister has left me to do all the work by myself? Tell her to help me!"

A hush came over the jovial party. Everyone turned to hear what Jesus would say.

"My dear Martha," Jesus said, reaching out and taking one of her trembling hands. "Why don't you sit down and rest as well? This party is beautiful, and the food will keep. You are worried and upset over all these details, but few things are really necessary for tonight. In fact, there's only one really important thing to do, and that is to learn more about God. And there is so much to learn!"

Jesus let go of her hand and motioned for her to take a seat on the floor next to Mary. "Mary has chosen what is better, dear Martha. This time with Me cannot be taken away from her."

Martha put her hands on her hips and looked ready to protest. But on second thought, she sank into a pillow next to Mary, exhaling loudly.

"There you go, friend," said Jesus. "Now, where was I?"

God Is **Knowable**

Martha became so overwhelmed with her list of jobs to get done, she forgot the most important thing of all—knowing Jesus. God is more interested in relationships than accomplishments. God wants to get to know you personally! He'd like to be friends with each one of us.

So how does a person get to know God? Where would you meet Him? What would you talk about?

First of all, He'll meet you anywhere you want. Just pick a spot! Knowing God isn't about where you go, it's about meeting with Him every day, reading His Word, and talking to Him about it. You can journal, pray, sing songs, talk out loud, take a walk—or just quietly sit in His presence. Don't worry about how He will answer you. You can be sure that He will.

~~~~~~~~~~~~~~~~~~~~~~~~~~~~~~~~~~~~~

13

God Is
the True Leader

If any of you wants to be my follower, you must turn from your selfish ways, take up your cross, and follow me. If you try to hang on to your life, you will lose it. But if you give up your life for my sake, you will save it.

MATTHEW 16:24-25

Trust in the LORD with all your heart; do not depend on your own understanding. Seek his will in all you do, and he will show you which path to take.

PROVERBS 3:5-6

The Battle of Jericho
Joshua 5-6

Moses was the first leader of the nation of Israel, and he would always be known as one of the very best. When he died, his younger assistant, Joshua, became the new leader of the Israelite people. God must have known Joshua needed encouragement in his new position, because this was the first thing He told him: "I command you—be strong and courageous! Don't be afraid or discouraged, for I will be with you wherever you go."

Joshua felt a lot better...until God revealed Joshua's first leadership challenge—to conquer the city of Jericho.

"Just how are we going to do that, God?" Joshua asked.

Monstrously thick walls surrounded the city of Jericho. The city gates were closed tightly and braced from the inside. Even if the Israelites were to surround Jericho and cut off its food supply, the city had enough stored up to last for years—and its own source of water. It was virtually impenetrable.

Joshua sat down to think. The people were counting on him to provide guidance and direction, just as Moses had. That was a lot of pressure! He chewed on the inside of his cheek while he drew a rough sketch of Jericho and calculated the height of the walls. Then he got out a separate sheet of paper and wrote down every strategy he could think of to attack Jericho: ladders, ropes, catapults, flaming arrows, poison darts, battering rams...

Three pages later, Joshua called for his assistant. "Collect every sword in camp and sharpen it. Get all the shields too, and make sure they have no weak spots." Joshua handed him his outline. "Then divide the men into groups and get them the supplies they'll need to build these things."

Joshua hadn't yet chosen a battle plan, but he wanted his army to be ready for anything!

~

The Israelite camp soon hummed with activity. Some men lashed ladders together, and others constructed mechanical catapults. Joshua congratulated the men on their hard work as he moved from station to station, overseeing their progress.

Then God whispered in his ear. "Joshua! You've done a great job organizing the troops. Your weapons are coming along great! But we're going to win this battle My way. I want you to march your army around the city once a day for six days."

"Okay," agreed Joshua. "Sounds good. Marching is fine. We can move the catapults into position while the people of Jericho are distracted by the parade."

"No," God countered. "Forget the catapults. Just march."

"O...kay..." Joshua said. "We'll march with our swords drawn so they glitter in the sunlight. Yeah, that will intimidate them! And then, *bam*—we'll shoot a few thousands flaming arrows!"

"No," God said. "No catapults, no swords, no arrows. I just want you to march around Jericho for six days. Then, on the seventh day, tell the priests to march ahead of the troops while playing their trumpets. Go around the city seven times."

"Hold on...trumpets?" Joshua sputtered. "Don't You want us to use the battering ram instead?"

"Are you having a hard time hearing Me, Joshua?" God asked.

"Well...no..."

"I didn't think so," God said. "I said trumpets, and that's what I meant. When the army is finished marching, the priests are to give one long blast. Then everybody is to shout as loud as he can. I want to hear volume! What do you think happens then?"

Joshua scratched his head. He nervously rolled his ankle back and forth. "Ladders and ropes?"

"No. The walls around Jericho will tumble down to the ground!"

For a moment, Joshua stood tongue-tied in the middle of Israel's

army camp. No flaming arrows? No siege ramps? He felt like pro-
testing. How could a war be won without poison darts?

"This is My victory," God reminded him.

"Your victory."

"That's right! You got it!" God said.

"Okay, fine. You win." Joshua lifted his hands in worship. "We'll do
this Your way, God."

Many soldiers had been watching Joshua's strange behavior and
hearing his seemingly one-sided conversation, but Joshua didn't
stop to explain. He simply turned and walked to his tent. He sat at
his desk and cleared away his drawings of Jericho, his battle plans,
and his lists of weaponry. Leave it to God to conquer a city with a
bunch of noise!

Joshua knew he might have a hard time explaining a daily march
around Jericho to his warriors. But if that was how God wanted
to win a victory, who was he to question it? Hadn't God done
even greater miracles during Israel's exodus from Egypt? Hadn't
He sustained them with heavenly manna, water from a rock,

and quail? The catalogue of God's miracles went on and on. So what if God's latest plan included a parade, brass horns, and yelling—Joshua knew he had nothing to fear. With God as his leader, everything was possible.

God Is the True Leader

God filled Joshua with strength and courage because Joshua chose to trust Him as the ultimate leader. When we take time to study God's Word and listen to His voice, we can be assured of the same leadership in our own lives. God says so in Proverbs 3:5-6.

When you take time to speak with God every day, His voice will be easier and easier for you to hear. So when something important comes up, you don't have to panic or wonder how to reach God. He's already right beside you.

Be strong and courageous! God is ready to fight your battles for you, just as He did for Joshua.

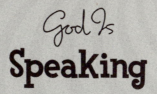

God Is Speaking

*Look! I stand at the door and knock. If you hear
my voice and open the door, I will come in, and
we will share a meal together as friends.*

REVELATION 3:20

Who's Talking?
1 Samuel 2-3

As far as Samuel was concerned, some days just stank.

Samuel understood that serving at the tabernacle under Eli the priest was a great privilege, but he was still only 12 years old! He looked outside on sunny days and wished he could join the neighborhood boys in their street games. Instead, he lived and worked daily at the temple, learning the ways of the priesthood alongside Eli's sons, Hophni and Phinehas.

Too bad those two were years older and no fun. Besides that, they were downright wicked. Every time Eli's back was turned, they were causing trouble—flirting with the women during church and stealing from the people's ceremonial offerings of food and money. Whenever Hophni spotted Samuel watching, he drew an ominous slash across his throat and pointed at him, letting Samuel know he'd be in big trouble if he tattled.

"Did you see something?" Hophni would challenge. "Whatcha gonna do about it, temple baby?"

Samuel sighed as he brushed his teeth before bed. Just thinking about those two exhausted him. He wished he could erase them from his mind, but Hophni and Phinehas were hard to ignore! Even now, long after the lights were out, they were listening to loud music and whooping it up just down the hall. In the temple!

Telling Eli would do no good. Samuel would pay dearly for snitching, and Eli wouldn't do anything anyway. The strongest reprimand Samuel had ever heard from Eli was, "Hey, you two, stop that and straighten up." Hophni and Phinehas had waited until Eli turned his back before crossing their eyes and sticking out their tongues.

Samuel shoved a cotton ball in each ear to drown out the noise, blew out his bedside candle, and crawled between his sheets. That was that. The sanctuary lantern glowed under his door—a comforting sight on another uncomfortably loud night.

Around two in the morning—at least Samuel suspected it was about that time—he awoke with a start. Total silence. He turned over and concentrated on the light under the door. Was someone in the sanctuary? What had awoken him? Sensing nothing, he closed his eyes again.

Moments later, he clearly heard a voice calling him—loud and distinct through his cotton-ball earplugs.

"Samuel! Samuel!"

Samuel sat straight up in bed and tore the earplugs out. He jumped out of bed, skipped over his slippers, and ran straight to Eli's room.

"Eli!" Samuel shook the priest. "What's wrong? I heard you call and I came as fast as I could!"

Eli rubbed his eyes and put a hand out in front of his face, "Eh? Who's there? Is someone there? What time is it?"

"It's me, Samuel, and it's the middle of the night. I heard you calling me and came as fast as I could."

"You must have been dreaming," said Eli, waving Samuel away. "Go back to bed, boy."

Eli turned over to go back to sleep, and Samuel padded slowly back toward his room. He was sure he had heard a voice—a very serious voice. Could it have been Phinehas? Phinehas did like to play pranks. One time he had put a toad in the bell of one of the temple trumpets. When it was time to worship and the toad jumped out, the trumpet player nearly wet his pants! With that in mind, Samuel crept into his room on guard, checking behind his door and under his bed.

The coast was clear. And no booby traps.

Samuel shut his door, latching it behind him. He jumped into bed, burrowing under the blankets, and began to quietly count backward from one hundred. He had just reached five when the voice called his name again.

"Samuel! Samuel!"

Exasperated, Samuel threw back the covers and tucked his feet into his slippers. *Eli is losing it!* Obviously he wanted something.

He grabbed his candle for better visibility and started down the hall.

Samuel knocked quietly on Eli's door before pushing it open. "Yes, Eli? You called?"

"Who's there?" cried Eli, bolting upright in bed. He squinted his eyes, "Samuel, is that you again?"

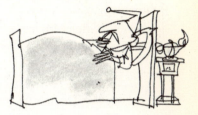

"Yes, sir. Here I am; you called."

"No, I didn't!" said Eli. "Is this some kind of joke? Scaring me out of my skin in the middle of the night?"

"Not at all, sir! I just heard—"

"You're making things up. Go back to bed." Again, Eli waved him off and lay down.

More confused than ever, Samuel backed out of the room.

"Shut the door tight, please," Eli called. Samuel did.

Maybe I'm getting sick, thought Samuel. *Maybe I'm delusional!* He didn't bother checking his room for pranks this time. He just leaped into bed and pressed his hands against his ears. *I'll be all right...I'll be all right*, he repeated to himself. *I'm not hearing things!*

"Samuel!"

This time the urgency of the call frightened Samuel. He ran. The old man must really be in trouble!

113

"Eli!" Samuel careened around the corner and burst through Eli's bedroom door. "I'm not making this up! You're calling me, aren't you! Are you okay?"

"Now you listen here—" But then Eli stopped and slowly raised himself onto one elbow, looking intently into Samuel's face. "You're not kidding with me, are you?"

"No sir. I've clearly heard you call me three times."

"Samuel, my boy, I'm not the one calling you." Eli pushed himself into a sitting position. "But I do know who is—God! He's talking to you, Samuel." Eli's face wrinkled into a sleepy smile. "God is talking to you! Now go back and lie down in your bed. If God calls you again, say, 'Yes, Lord, I'm listening.'"

Awestruck, Samuel jogged back to his room and lay down. He didn't have long to wait. God came and stood before him, calling, "Samuel! Samuel!"

Quivering with fear, Samuel peeked over the bedcovers and responded as Eli had instructed. "Yes, Lord, I'm listening."

"Samuel, this news might make you a bit uncomfortable, but it's the truth. I'm bringing judgment on Eli's family. I've warned Eli time and time again to discipline Hophni and Phinehas, but nothing's come of it, and I've reached my limit. There will be consequences."

Then God left.

Of course, Samuel couldn't sleep after that! He sat up wide-eyed in his bed, chewing over the unhappy news until he absolutely had to open the temple doors for morning services. Two emotions warred inside him—awe because he heard God's voice, and fear because he had bad news to deliver.

Eli saw him slumping through his morning duties. "Samuel, God spoke to you again last night, didn't He. What did He tell you? Don't you dare hide anything from me! Tell me exactly what He said, even if you think it might hurt my feelings."

Samuel couldn't help but burst into tears as he repeated word for word what God had told him. Judgment on Eli's family was coming! Eli quietly nodded, and his shoulders sagged.

"It is all true," he concluded. "Every word. He is the Lord. Let Him do what is good in His eyes."

From that day forward, God continued to speak to Samuel, and the people who heard him recognized that he was a true prophet of the Lord. Some sunny afternoons Samuel still stared out the temple windows, wishing he could join other kids playing outside...but then the memory of God's voice echoed in his head, and he trembled at the thought that God had chosen to speak to the nation of Israel through him. Him! That was even better than kickball.

 God Is **Speaking**

God wants to talk to you. Are you ready to hear from Him? Would you know His voice if He spoke to you? Do you have time to listen? If you want to hear what God is saying, pursue a relationship with Him. Then when He speaks, you'll recognize His voice—and He will tell you incredible things.

15

God Is
the Ultimate Judge

When [Jesse's sons] arrived, Samuel took one look at Eliab and thought, "Surely this is the LORD's anointed!" But the LORD said to Samuel, "Don't judge by his appearance or height, for I have rejected him. The LORD doesn't see things the way you see them! People judge by outward appearance, but the LORD looks at the heart."

1 SAMUEL 16:6-7

This Guy?
1 Samuel 16

Samuel, God's prophet and priest, paced the length of his living room, shaking his head and harrumphing. *Of all the things to happen, why this?* he thought. *Why me? Why now?*

"Samuel!" God said. "Stop it! How long are you going to mope around your house wishing King Saul would straighten up? He's not going to, and I have rejected him. It is time for a new king in Israel. Get your anointing oil and go to Bethlehem. The next king of Israel is one of Jesse's sons."

Samuel recalled anointing Saul many years ago. He was a handsome young man, bursting with potential and goodwill when he became king of Israel. What a day that had been! Israel's first king had made quite an impression on the people...but now that memory was tarnished by King Saul's rebellious disobedience.

"Saul will not take his crown off willingly," Samuel said. "When he finds out what I'm going to do, he will certainly kill me."

"Then take a cow with you," God replied. "Tell everyone in Bethlehem that you have come to make a sacrifice to the Lord. Invite Jesse and his family to the sacrifice, and I'll point out which son you will anoint for Me."

So Samuel did exactly what God said.

When he arrived in Bethlehem, the entire city came to the sacrifice and shared a big meal. After dinner, Samuel asked if he might be introduced to the sons of Jesse. Honored, Jesse lined up his boys from oldest to youngest and instructed each to present himself to Samuel by stepping forward and announcing his name.

The first young man to come forward was tall and strikingly handsome. "Eliab," he declared, bowing deeply.

Samuel nodded enthusiastically and patted the young man on his shoulders. Surely this was the chosen son! He reached for his oil.

"No," God said sternly in Samuel's ear. "This is not the boy. He may be attractive and appear kingly to you, but I'm not looking for someone handsome, Samuel. Don't be impressed with what's on the outside. I'm looking at people's hearts."

Samuel quickly tucked the anointing oil back in his robe and
moved down the line, motioning for the next boy's introduction.
Jesse pushed forward his second son, Abinadab. Samuel listened
for God's instructions but heard nothing.

"No, you're not the one," Samuel said kindly as he called for the
third son.

Shimea was another tall and good-looking young man who in
every way resembled a royal youth. He stepped forward, but no,
God had not chosen Shimea either. Samuel patiently went down
the line, meeting Jesse's other four sons.

"Are these all the sons you have?"

Jesse blushed. "Well, no...but the youngest is out in the fields
tending the sheep."

"Well, go get him!" Samuel said. "Nothing more will happen until
he gets here!"

Jesse immediately ordered one of his field hands to run
and collect his youngest son, David. The two of
them came back sweaty and out of breath,
having just run three miles in the
heat of the
day.

Samuel hesitated as he looked
at David. This one? David had
flushed cheeks and rugged fea-
tures. He wore the clothes of a shepherd
and carried a staff and a small harp. His hair
bent off his head every which way, giving him a rather wild look.
David gave his father a big hug.

"What's the big emergency?"

Jesse bit his lip and turned David about, facing Samuel. "Samuel the priest is here to worship with us today, son. Please, show some respect."

David stepped forward and bowed politely before Samuel. "Thank you for honoring us with your presence, sir."

As Samuel lay his hand on David's head, he heard the voice of God, "This is the one—My chosen king!"

Samuel nodded to himself and removed the anointing oil from his pocket. "David," he said, "you have been chosen by God Himself to be the next king of Israel." He uncorked the small vial of oil and poured its entire contents over David's head. The golden liquid ran down his forehead, flowed over his cheeks, and dripped from his chin.

Jesse stood nearby, stunned.

"Me?" David mouthed, astonished.

"Him?" questioned Jesse.

"Yes," confirmed Samuel. "God has made His choice. David will be king."

~

King David walked faithfully with the Lord all the days of his life. He was much more than a shepherd-boy turned king. His life was

full of adventure and intrigue, battles and prayer. David also wrote music, played the harp, and penned most of the book of Psalms. Best of all, he loved the Lord with all of his heart.

God Is **the Ultimate Judge**

Have you ever judged a person before you got to know him? Most of us have. We make our first impressions in three to five seconds— that's not even long enough to introduce yourself! We judge people incorrectly all the time. God is the only judge who never gets it wrong. His justice is absolute, and His remedies are forever.

Aren't you glad God takes more than three seconds to get to know you? He looks at your heart.

(To discover more about King David's astounding life, turn to 1 Samuel and 2 Samuel in your Bible.)

16

God Is
Wisdom

My child, listen to what I say, and treasure my commands. Tune your ears to wisdom, and concentrate on understanding. Cry out for insight, and ask for understanding. Search for them as you would for silver; seek them like hidden treasures. Then you will understand what it means to fear the LORD, and you will gain knowledge of God. For the LORD grants wisdom! From his mouth come knowledge and understanding. He grants a treasure of common sense to the honest. He is a shield to those who walk with integrity. He guards the paths of the just and protects those who are faithful to him. Then you will understand what is right, just, and fair, and you will find the right way to go. For wisdom will enter your heart, and knowledge will fill you with joy.

PROVERBS 2:1-10

Wisdom Speaks

1 Kings 3

It took about three minutes for Solomon to figure out that being the king of Israel wasn't going to be easy—at all. He thought getting along with his brothers and sisters was hard, but getting along with other countries? Way over his head. Add all of his family's drama and his father's recent death, and Solomon couldn't sleep at night.

Thankfully, Solomon knew what to do. He prayerfully took his problems to God. It took all day long to thoroughly explain every issue from the greatest to least importance, and when he had finished, he could only manage to say one word over and over again: "Help! Help, help, help!"

That night, God appeared to Solomon in a dream.

HELP!

"Solomon! I've heard your concerns. What is it that you want most? Ask me and I'll give it to you," God said.

"O God!" replied Solomon. "Please give me the wisdom to govern Your people! I need the ability to tell right from wrong. How else am I going to make it as Israel's king?"

124

God beamed. "Good choice! I'm proud of you. Because you've asked for understanding instead of money or popularity, I'm going to give you so much more. I'll give you greater wisdom than any man born before or after you—and I'll give you riches too!"

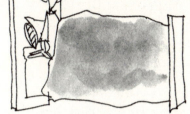

When Solomon awoke, peace filled his heart. Gone were the sleepless nights and nail-biting study sessions. Family drama no longer dominated his every waking hour. Instead, God filled Solomon with supernatural understanding and insight so he could govern the people and help them solve their problems.

~

His first big test came during a civic ruling session. Two women arrived at the palace, bickering and stirring up trouble. Despite the palace aides' best attempts to quietly lead them into the courtroom, they argued all the way down the marble hallway and through the gilded doors. As soon as they saw King Solomon, one of the women broke free and rushed the throne. Her name was Ruby.

"O King Solomon, you must help us!" Ruby pleaded, throwing herself at his feet. "Sheila and I are roommates, and we both got pregnant and gave birth to babies within a week of one another. Then one night, the most horrible thing happened—Sheila rolled over on her baby, and it died! I was still asleep and didn't know what had happened, and that's when she—" Ruby's voice cracked into a sob. "She took my baby and replaced it with her own dead son! When I awoke to nurse my baby in the morning, I was appalled to find her dead child in my arms—and my living baby in hers. She claims I'm crazy and that it was my baby who died, but I know my own flesh and blood! I do!"

"Liar!" shouted Sheila, shoving Ruby out of the way. "That's not at all what happened, King Solomon! The dead child is hers. Mine is the one who is still alive."

"Not true!" hiccuped Ruby. "My baby is alive and yours is dead!"

"Liar, liar, pants on fire!" Sheila screamed.

"Oooh, you are an evil, evil woman," cried Ruby. "Why you—"

"Enough!" called King Solomon, silencing the two women. "Let me understand this. Sheila, you say that the living child is yours and the dead one belongs to Ruby."

Sheila nodded.

"And Ruby, you claim that Sheila replaced your living son with her own dead baby."

"Yes," whispered Ruby through her tears.

"Okay then," continued the king, "this is really quite simple. Bring me a sword!"

Immediately a long, sharp blade was presented to King Solomon.

He turned it over a few times before making a swift slice through the air inches from the women's noses.

They gasped.

"I'm going to cut the living baby in half," he said, motioning for the infant to be brought before him. "This way, each of you will have part of him. Fifty-fifty."

The baby boy was laid on King Solomon's stone desk, where he cooed and gurgled, squirming to get out of his swaddling clothes. King Solomon stood up and raised the sword over his head.

Ruby clutched her throat with a half-swallowed cry. She fell over the baby to shield him from the blow. "Stop!" she yelled. "Don't divide the baby! Give him to Sheila and forget I was ever here!"

Instead of saying thank you, Sheila crossed her arms against her chest and raised her chin, "Make it fifty-fifty! Then it's fair—neither of us will have a baby!"

Solomon lowered his sword slowly. "Sheila, you are certainly not this boy's mother." He lifted the small baby, adjusting his swaddling clothes and blowing kisses into his face. "This baby belongs to Ruby. Here you go," he said, handing the baby over to his true mother.

Ruby cradled her baby to her chest. "Thank you, King Solomon. Thank you."

Sheila, on the other hand, clenched her fists and spat on the white marble floor. She glowered at the king and then at Ruby.

"I hate you both!" she snarled. Immediately two guards escorted her through the double doors at the rear of the courtroom.

King Solomon sadly watched Sheila's removal. "Ruby," he said, "this is a great turning point in your life. It's time to start over."

Ruby nodded, wiping away her tears.

"I also suggest," said the king, "that you find a new roommate."

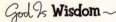 ## God Is **Wisdom**

What do you want most of all? Do you treasure wisdom, just as King Solomon did? The Bible says wisdom is more precious than rubies. So how do you gain wisdom?

Psalm 111:10 tells us, "Fear of the LORD is the foundation of true wisdom." God wants to give all His children the gift of understanding. We only have to ask for it and be prepared to receive. Ask for wisdom today!

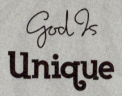

17

God Is
Unique

*I am the L*ORD*; that is my name! I will not give my glory
to anyone else, nor share my praise with carved idols.*

ISAIAH 42:8

There Is Only One
1 Samuel 4–5

Israel's army headquarters buzzed with debate. The Philistines were crushing them in every engagement, and today's defeat had been particularly humiliating.

"What are we missing?" asked General Abrams. "We have more troops, we're better prepared, and we have inside intel on their tactics! Today's slaughter is an embarrassment. It should never have happened!"

The Israeli leadership melted in the stuffy tent, sweating over their conference table in the late afternoon heat.

"Yes," agreed Colonel Lerner, wiping his brow. "Four thousand of our troops died today for no good reason."

The men stared at the failed battle plan. No one spoke as the gruesome reality of their losses sunk in.

"I'll tell you what happened," said Lieutenant

Colonel Meir, slamming his fist into the table. "We lost this battle because we've lost God's favor!" The men were silent, each considering the explanation thoughtfully.

But General Abrams had a different viewpoint. "Maybe we just need God closer. We should bring the Ark of the Covenant here to the battlefield. We can't lose with God fighting for us. And the Ark will rally the troops."

After a thoughtful pause, the small group of commanders began clapping.

"Wonderful idea!"

"Can't believe we didn't think of it before!"

"First-rate!"

But not everyone thought the idea was a good one. Major General Brenner sat with his arms crossed across his chest until the others finished applauding.

"With all respect, sir, bringing the Ark of the Covenant here to the battlefield is a terrible idea," he said, standing. "Surely you realize that our God isn't in that box. Our God cannot be manipulated. We can't require Him to do what we want! If we've lost God's favor, we should be asking Him why we've lost His favor and how we can gain it back again."

General Abrams waved off Major General Brenner's assessment and shook his head dismissively. "Lost His favor? Impossible— we're God's chosen people."

"That doesn't guarantee success! God's not in the Ark!" argued Major General Brenner.

General Abrams ignored Brenner and addressed the rest of the room. "Let's get a consensus here. Who says bring the Ark?" he asked. "Raise your hand."

"Aye!"

"Seconded!"

"Bring the Ark!"

So that's just what happened.

Two temple priests, Hophni and Phinehas, were called to bring the Ark of the Covenant to the front lines. They placed the Ark on the top of a small rise so everyone on both sides of the battlefield could clearly see it.

With the Ark of the Covenant displayed behind them, General Abrams called for a frontal assault on the Philistines. The Israelite infantry charged into the Philistine ranks, followed closely by their most elite soldiers.

A thunderous rumble ensued. Battle-hardened warriors slashed their way through the front lines with arcing swords and drawn bows. The sounds of trumpets, war cries, and screams filled the battlefield. Israel's standard flew high above the struggle, staged on the hill next to the Ark of the Covenant.

Despite their fervor, 30,000 Israeli soldiers lay dead across the battlefield at the end of the day. General Abrams frantically waved a white flag, while behind him, the hallowed Ark of the Covenant rattled off to enemy territory in a handcart pulled by Philistine militiamen.

The loss sent a clear message to the Israeli leadership—God would not be manipulated or used for anyone's glorification but His own.

After a final vote, the Philistine leaders decided to place the Ark of the Covenant in the temple of Dagon in the great city of Ashdod.

The symbolism was obvious—the Ark would rest at Dagon's feet, showing that the Philistines' god had triumphed over the Israelites' God.

The day after the ark arrived in Ashdod, crowds of Philistines pushed their way toward the temple of Dagon. Work and school had been canceled so that everyone could celebrate the victory. Confetti filled the air, and sidewalk bands popped up on every corner to play the Philistine national anthem. At the temple of Dagon, priests opened the double doors, inviting the entire community inside.

Within moments of entering the temple, the first visitors backed out so quickly that they knocked down the people behind them! White-faced, they murmured a fearful message that spread through the crowded streets—Dagon lay facedown on the floor!

Indeed, the Philistine god had fallen in front of the Ark of the Covenant. Temple workers rushed to lift Dagon to his rightful place of prestige and attempted to quiet the worries outside.

"It doesn't mean anything," said the temple priest. "Come back tomorrow and we'll really celebrate."

The next morning an even greater mass of people pressed against Dagon's temple gates. When the doors were unlocked, the people overwhelmed the priests, swarming inside. But once again, the people immediately backed away. Panicked men and women shrieked and pulled their hair. Earsplitting wails spread from the temple gates!

"He has fallen again!"

"His head is severed!"

"His hands are broken off!"

This news was even more devastating than the news of the day before because the severed head and hands of enemy soldiers were considered war trophies. Dagon lay mutilated before the Ark of the Covenant, a clear symbol of God's superiority.

Dagon's priests slammed shut the temple gates and locked the doors behind the mob.

~

That afternoon, a stillness like a thick fog settled over the city of Ashdod. People hid in their homes, covering their windows and talking in whispers. What had happened in the temple was no fluke—it was a sign! What grim omen would come next?

The citizens of Ashdod didn't have long to wait.

At dusk, a great horde of rats descended from the hills. Twenty thousand or more swarmed the streets of Ashdod, slipping under doors and through cracks in walls. Where one rat found a small opening, ten more would follow! The rats gnawed and ate everything in their path. They infested the food stores, scattering and eating all they wanted. They chewed holes in the people's clothes and nibbled on their toes. No home was safe and no place secure.

Disease followed the crushing flood of rodents. Some people died from bites and infection while others developed painful tumors. And they knew why they were suffering all these problems.

"The Ark must leave!"

"Today! Send it away today!"

"Dagon cannot save us!"

The next morning an angry mob assembled at the city square. They marched around the block with signs reading "Ark-B-Gone!" "Tumor-row is too late!" and "Take the Ark, take the rats!" They screamed until they were hoarse.

News of disease and chaos in the city of Ashdod unnerved the Philistine rulers. They instructed the governor of Ashdod to have the Ark of the Covenant moved before rumors of the Ark's supernatural powers reached any other city.

"Place it in Gath," they said. "And disband your protestors immediately."

People in the city of Gath hadn't heard anything about Ashdod's troubles, so they were overjoyed to receive the Ark of the Covenant! Finally, something that their little town could brag about!

And they did, celebrating and dancing in the streets—that is, until an identical swarm of rats coiled around the city, bringing death and tumors to the people.

The Ark of the Covenant was quickly transported away to the Philistine city of Ekron.

As soon as the cart carrying the Ark passed through Ekron's city gates, a great cry went up among the people. "Our own rulers are trying to kill us by bringing the Ark here! Get it away! Move it out! Don't let it come in!" For even as the cart rolled down the street, the army of rats followed close behind, darting down side streets, through homes, and into businesses, schools, and temples. Clearly, God intended to show His power in Ekron just as He had in Gath and Ashdod.

People started to riot because they were angry and afraid, so the Philistine governors securely fastened the Ark of the Covenant to a wooden cart pulled by two young cows. They pointed the cows toward pastureland and sent them off.

"This is the true test of Israel's God!" said one of the governors. "Let's see if it takes itself home!"

"Yes," agreed another, "this will show the people that Israel's God is not so powerful after all. The disease, the rats, the statue of Dagon...it's all been bad luck. A coincidence! These two cows have nursing calves in the barn. They won't go anywhere."

Yet the two cows took the Ark of the Covenant straight through their pastureland, past their barn and nursing calves. They didn't turn right or left. The cows lumbered onto the highway to Israel and never turned back.

God Is *Unique*

The Israelites thought they could manipulate God into winning their battle for them. The Philistines thought their fake god, Dagon, was more powerful than the Almighty God. Both sides were wrong! God cannot be manipulated or used. He will not share His glory with anyone else. He will not share His praise with idols.

18

God Is
Our Provider

Don't be concerned about what to eat and what to drink.
Don't worry about such things. These things dominate
the thoughts of unbelievers all over the world, but your
Father already knows your needs. Seek the Kingdom of God
above all else, and he will give you everything you need.

LUKE 12:29-31

Teach those who are rich in this world not to be
proud and not to trust in their money, which is so
unreliable. But their trust should be in God, who
richly gives us all we need for our enjoyment.

1 TIMOTHY 6:17

The Widow and Her Son
1 Kings 17

The drought continued.

Month after month, year after year, not a drop of rain hit the ground. Even the wilderness brook where the prophet Elijah hid from evil King Ahab dried up. The entire country was very, very thirsty.

Elijah packed his few belongings and headed toward the coast. God told him that a widow woman would care for him in the town of Zarephath.

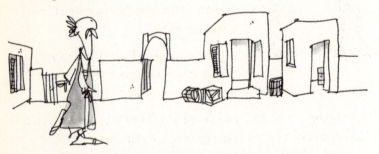

When Elijah arrived, the city streets were deserted. The people had nowhere to go, no food to eat, and very little water to drink. Elijah sat down next to the town gate and waited for the widow to appear as God had said she would.

Before long, Elijah saw a tiny woman making her way through the withering orange trees near the wall. She was bent over, laboring to scoop together handfuls of tiny sticks. Though her basket was only half-full of the scrappy twigs, she carried it as if it weighed twice her weight. She was beyond thin—just a shadow of a person, hobbling through the orchard.

"Woman!" called Elijah.

She did not turn around.

"Hello?" he tried again.

No response. Elijah got up and walked toward her.

"Miss?" he said. Her cracked lips, red swollen eyes, and shrunken cheeks pained Elijah.

"Who, me?" she asked.

"Yes," Elijah started. "I'm a prophet of the Most High God. He has sent me here to Zarephath. Might I trouble you for a drink of water?"

"I can only offer you a little," replied the woman. "We distill the sea water, but it still tastes salty."

"Anything is fine," Elijah said. "I'm very thirsty. And...if it's not too much to ask, may I have a piece of bread too? I haven't eaten in days."

"That I cannot give you," said the widow. "I swear by the Lord your God that I don't have a single piece of bread in the house. And I have only a handful of flour left in the jar and a little cooking oil in the bottom of the jug. I was just gathering a few sticks to cook this last meal, and then my son and I will die."

She said the last sentence with such finality that Elijah's eyes filled with tears. He took her basket and offered her his arm for support.

"Dear woman, don't be afraid. Go ahead and cook your meal, but bake me a little loaf of bread first. Afterward, I promise, there will still be enough food for you and your son. For this is what the Lord, the God of Israel, says: 'There will always be plenty of flour and oil left in your containers until the Lord sends rain and the crops grow again!'"

The widow woman lowered her eyes. She was not an Israelite. Why would one of their prophets promise her a miraculous supply of food in return for her last loaf of bread? Oh well, she thought, what does it matter? She had nothing left in her cupboards, so regardless of whether she and her son ate anything tonight, they would still starve in a week. Shrugging her shoulders, she motioned for Elijah to follow her home. She would give this prophet her last meal.

The widow's son took Elijah's coat and hung it over the back of a chair, welcoming him to sit at a table in their small kitchen. The widow poured her final cup of flour into a tiny mound on the table. She dribbled the last of the oil on top and kneaded the dough into a pocket-sized cake before putting it in the wood-fire oven to bake. Soon the warm smell of homemade bread filled the small house. All three of their stomachs rumbled in anticipation.

"There you are," she said to Elijah, setting the toasted bun before him. "Enjoy."

"Where's your bread? And your son's?" asked Elijah. "Certainly you and the boy are also hungry for dinner."

"As I told you outside," said the widow, "I have no more oil and flour. That bread is the last meal anyone will eat in this house."

Elijah pushed the plate away and leaned over the table. "I told you that my God is going to provide. So I'll wait to eat this delicious roll until your bread is done too."

Elijah relaxed back in his seat and crossed his arms. The widow stared at him, confused. Her son, however, was hungry and desperate to eat something. He grabbed the flour container and upended it on the table. Out poured two handfuls of flour—enough for two more bread rolls!

"Mother!" cried the boy. "There is flour!"

The widow looked dubiously at the mound of flour. "We'll still be needing oil, and I know I used all of it."

The boy hefted the jug of cooking oil and turned it over too. Out poured half a cup of oil!

"Oil!" shouted the boy. "We can make bread!"

"Incredible," mumbled the woman, tenderly touching the heap of flour and oil before her. Then she dug her hands in, kneading the dough hungrily. "Who *are* you?" she questioned Elijah.

"I'm a prophet of the one true God. As I said before, He is going to provide for you and your son. There will always be plenty of flour and oil left in your containers until the time when the Lord sends rain and the crops grow again."

A spark of hope lit up the little kitchen in Zarephath. For the first time in months, the widow and her son laughed together as they shared a meal.

Elijah continued to live with the widow and her son. Every day, the widow made bread for the three of them, never running low on flour or oil, just as God had promised.

God Is Our Provider

God is the ultimate provider.

The widow had never met God, who had the power to provide for her in her most desperate hour of need. Thankfully, Elijah introduced her to Him. Our God promises to provide for us. He cares deeply about you! Turn to Him in your need and watch what He can do.

19

God Is

Our Only Source of True Strength

The people will declare, "The LORD is the source of all my righteousness and strength."

ISAIAH 45:24

The Strongman

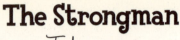

Judges 13-16

To say Samson was strong would be an understatement. Samson was unnaturally, superhumanly strong. Samson's parents dedicated him to God as a Nazarite before his birth, so they never cut his hair because it symbolized God's supernatural strength in him.

Samson couldn't help being a little vain. He was handsome and well built, and he could rip the Palestine Seacoast phone book right in half before he turned six. When he was eight, he took to bending iron bars. When he was fifteen, he killed a lion with his own bare hands! No one messed with Samson. No one had ever seen muscles like his!

When Samson turned 21, he went to the city of Gaza for a birthday celebration. While he was there, he met a very beautiful Philistine woman named Delilah at a local hot spot. They danced, they told each other jokes, and Samson tried his best to impress her by lifting two full dining tables into the air, one in each hand.

"Oh, Samson!" Delilah gushed, batting her long black eyelashes. "You are sooo strong and handsome. I hope we can date!"

Samson dropped the tables right there.

"Date you? Why, I'd love to!" he said, and smooched her on the cheek. "You're gorgeous—and just my type. What do you say we go someplace a little more private..."

"Now, now," she said, pushing him back with the tips of her fingers. "Don't be hasty! You just stay right here, and I'll be right back." Delilah flipped her long dark hair over her shoulders and sashayed into the powder room. Samson couldn't help but stare.

Once in the bathroom, Delilah hiked up her skirts and climbed on top of the sink. She pushed open the window and whistled the melodious call of the nightingale. A man crouching below the window ledge answered.

"Delilah, you're late."

"Woman's work takes time, dear cousin," she replied. "Don't rush me."

"You've been trying to catch his attention for weeks! There's no payday for flirting," he said. "Only for the answer to his strength."

"I know that!" Delilah replied. "I'm working on it! I'll find out what makes him so strong, don't you worry. But now that I've got his attention, no more following me around. He might notice. I'll call for you when he's secured."

"Fine," said the man, getting up and brushing the dust from his pants. "Call me as soon as you can. And no dillydallying! This is serious business." The man disappeared into the night.

Delilah hopped off the sink and smoothed down her skirts. She wet her hands and ran them over her hair, brushing strays back into place. If it weren't for the 3300 shekels of silver she'd earn, this job would be history! She looked in the mirror, pinched her cheeks rosy, and plastered a fake smile on her face. He'd better crack soon.

~

Back at their table, Samson was in the middle of another feat of strength. The boisterous crowd counted along as he heaved 12 men sitting on a wooden plank into the air.

"Sixty-two! Sixty-three! Sixty-four!"

Delilah clapped her hands together, cooing from the sidelines. "Go, Samson! You're so strong!"

When he reached 100, the bar patrons erupted into thunderous applause, whoops, and hollers. Impressed, the bartender handed out a round on the house!

Samson pulled Delilah close and whispered in her ear. "Babe, that was nothing. I can do so much more!"

Delilah giggled. "Samson," she asked, running her hand along his bicep. "What is the secret to your strength?"

"My strength? Besides eating four dozen eggs a day, you mean?"

"Don't joke," she said. "I really want to know."

Samson's face got warm. She was so pretty, and she smelled nice too. He had never wanted to tell anyone his secret more, but he had promised his mother...

"Tell you what, if anyone tied me up with seven new bowstrings, well then, I'd be as helpless as a little lamb," he said, leaning in for a kiss.

"Oh no you don't, little lamb!" laughed Delilah. "You can't kiss me here! Let's go back to my house." She grabbed her purse and danced out the door. Samson followed, hypnotized.

~

In her kitchen, Delilah poured two glasses of wine while Samson relaxed on her couch. She secretly opened a small bottle and dropped a sleeping pill into Samson's glass, stirring it in with a spoon.

"Let's drink to good times," she said brightly as she entered the living room.

Samson eagerly took his glass and raised it high. "To good times and to the most beautiful woman on earth—Delilah!"

Delilah smiled. "Drink up and tell me about yourself."

Eager to impress, Samson recounted the time he raced a cheetah three miles before wrestling it to the ground. But just as he got to the good part, his glass slipped from his fingers, spilling on the floor. He looked at his hands, confused.

"Slippery little thing," he mumbled, reaching for the glass before slumping over the cushions. His eyes rolled back in his head, and his tongue lolled from the side of his mouth. Samson began to snore loudly.

"Well, that took long enough." Delilah rushed to the window.

A birdcall brought her cousin and two coconspirators out from the deep shadow across the street. "He's told me his secret. Go buy seven new bowstrings. And bring me my money."

The three Philistines returned with the cords and bound Samson head to toe. Then they hid in Delilah's coat closet, giddy with excitement. They were very close to bringing down Israel's most notorious strongman!

"Samson!" shouted Delilah. "The Philistines are here to capture you!"

Samson leapt from the couch, breaking the bowstrings as if they were threads. "Where!" he shouted. "Lemme at 'em!"

The men in the coat closet shuddered.

"How did this happen?" asked Delilah, picking up a broken bowstring. "Samson, I thought you said bowstrings were the secret to your strength!"

"Did I?" asked Samson, peeking through the front curtains into the dark streets below. "Did you see where they ran?"

"I'm serious!" pouted Delilah. "You told me you would be as helpless as a little lamb!" She sniffed. "You lied to me."

Samson turned from the window and smiled at Delilah. "Now, why would you want me as helpless as a little lamb and not as strong as an ox? Hmm? With me around, you don't have to worry about those pesky Philistines. I'll protect you." He flexed his muscles.

~

Two nights later, Samson invited Delilah out again. "Are you ready for the best second date of your life?" he asked.

Delilah averted her eyes. "You have a lot of nerve asking me out again! But I might consider going out with you again if you promise it won't be as embarrassing as the first date."

"Embarrassing?" asked Samson. "What are you talking about? Are you mad because I fell asleep on your couch? I still can't believe I did that. Let me make it up to you."

"Really?" Delilah perked up. "You mean it? Well...okay then, come on in for something to drink before dinner. Try not to fall asleep this time!"

~

Upstairs, Samson perched on the edge of Delilah's living-room couch, waiting for her to bring a glass of wine. He nervously wiped his hands on his pants and checked his watch for the third time. They still had 45 minutes until the dinner reservation. Samson wanted everything to go perfectly this time.

Delilah handed Samson his drink. "Samson, I think you should tell me the real secret to your strength this time. No fooling around—I really want to know."

Samson took a sip and winked. "I'll tell you what. If you'd used brand-new ropes instead of those bowstrings, I'd be as weak as any other man out there."

"New ropes, you say?" said Delilah. "Brand-new?"

"Fresh off...the rope...truck..." Samson said as his eyes rolled back in his head and he collapsed across the couch.

Delilah called her cousin again. "He's out," she said. "Bring brand-new ropes this time."

An hour later, the three men crouched once again behind the coat closet door while Delilah prepared to wake Samson. She spritzed herself with expensive perfume, adjusted her dress this way and that, and put on a pair of high heels. Then she bent over his reclining figure and yelled into his ear. "Samson! The Philistines are upon you!"

Samson slowly opened his eyes. "What?" he asked, groggy from the sleeping pills.

"The Philistines are upon you!"

"Philistines!" shouted Samson, leaping from the couch. The brand-new ropes popped and frayed as if they were made of cheap yarn.

He hefted Delilah's couch into the air and looked wildly about.

"I'll squash 'em! Where are they?"

"Samson!" pouted Delilah. "You lied to me again!" She burst into fake tears. Samson put down the couch and sat next to her.

"Why do you want to take away my strength?" he asked, lifting up her chin. "You already have me weak at the knees!" He brushed the hair out of her face and wiped the tears from her cheeks. Delilah continued pouting, her bottom lip protruding. She looked at him with pleading eyes.

"Oh, Delilah," said Samson, laughing, "you sure are a firecracker!" He hugged her tightly before checking his watch. "Oh no! I can't believe it! We've missed dinner again. When did I fall asleep? Baby, you should have woken me!"

Delilah rolled her neck, exasperated. "All you ever do is sleep!" she exploded. "And make a fool out of me! This is the second time you've lied to me, Samson of Dan! Look at you! You just stand there as if it's no big deal. As if lying to me is funny! Do you think this is funny? Do you?"

Samson's smile faded. "I'm so sorry, Delilah. How can I make it up to you? I didn't mean to make you feel foolish."

"Then tell me the secret to your strength!" Delilah fumed, stomping her foot.

"I can't."

"Why not?"

"It's a secret," said Samson.

"A secret? Come on! If we're going to date, I want to know everything about you. Everything. We shouldn't keep secrets."

Delilah came over to Samson and ran her fingers through his hair. "You have such beautiful hair, Samson. It must have taken ages to grow it this long. Let me brush it for you while you tell me about your strength."

Samson shivered. She was exquisite! He'd do just about anything to make her happy. He looked around the room, grasping for an explanation...and then he saw the weaving loom propped up against the far wall.

"Do you sew?" he asked.

"Sometimes. What of it?"

"Well, that's the answer," said Samson. "If you weaved my hair into that loom over there, I'd never be able to get out. I'd be your captive forever." Samson gazed into her eyes and begged for a kiss.

Delilah leaned in and gave him a peck on the cheek. "And I thought weaving was boring! Let's go get dinner!"

Delilah grabbed her purse and slung it over her shoulder. Samson followed her out the door like a puppy dog. When he got to the restaurant, he ate like one too, chowing down so fast he didn't notice the odd taste of his rice and beans. Before the dessert cart came by, Samson was holding his stomach and sweating through his shirt.

"I really don't feel well," said Samson, doubled over in pain. "I...I...I need to lie down."

"Oh, Samson...you don't look well either. Let me take care of you," cooed Delilah. "You can rest at my house!"

Back at her home, Delilah made Samson comfortable on her couch, propping his head up with a pillow and covering his clammy body with a thin blanket. She hummed a lullaby and brushed his hair. When his deep breathing became a quiet snore, Delilah gradually inched away from him, crept to the hall closet, and whispered through the doors.

"We've got him this time, boys."

While the three Philistines watched from their hiding place, Delilah placed her loom near Samson's head.

With special care, she began weaving his long hair into the threads, creating nearly a yard of fabric before sitting back, satisfied she had figured him out this time.

"The Philistines are com—"

Delilah didn't even finish her sentence before Samson was up and ready for a fight. The loom lay in ruins on the floor beside him.

"Again? You lied to me again?" Delilah's face flushed violet. "This is getting ridiculous, Samson! That's three times you've lied to me, and now look what you did! You've ruined my loom! It's just a pile of sticks! Now how am I going to make rugs and drapes and scarves?"

Confused, sweaty, and still more than a little sick, Samson shook his head. "You never give up, do you?"

"I thought you loved me!" cried Delilah. "I thought we were meant to be together! How can you say you love me when you won't tell me everything? How can I possibly return the love of a man who keeps secrets from me? Samson, are you listening to me? Samson...?"

Green faced, Samson doubled over and threw up on her carpet.

Delilah screamed.

Dizzy, Samson stumbled out of Delilah's apartment, down the stairs, and back to his own home.

~

Of course, a few days later when he started to feel better, Samson couldn't stop thinking about Delilah. He had broken her loom. He had fallen asleep on their dates. Maybe she did have a right to be mad at him! The next evening he stopped by her apartment to apologize.

"I'm really sorry about our last date," he said when she opened the door.

"Really?" questioned Delilah. "Which part?"

"Well, for starters, I threw up on your carpet."

"And?"

"And I guess I ruined your loom," he said.

"And?"

Samson just stared at her.

Delilah put a finger in his chest. "And you lied to me! Three times! I don't think I want to see you again." She began to shut her door.

"Wait," said Samson, stopping the door with his foot. "Don't say that. I...I love you."

Delilah cocked her head to one side and put a hand on her hip. "Love me? Really? Then tell me the source of your strength! What makes you so strong, Samson?"

"That's it?" he asked. "That's the most important part of our relationship?"

"Yes," she said. "I just can't trust the man I love if he can't tell me the truth about himself. If you told me the real secret to your strength, I'd marry you."

Samson's eyes grew wide. His heart pounded.

"Oh, Delilah," he said, pushing his way into her apartment. "I'll tell you, but you can't let anyone else know." He shut the door firmly behind him. "The secret to my strength is my hair. It's never been cut and never can be cut. My hair symbolizes God's strength in me. It's His power, not my own."

Delilah hugged Samson and kissed him. She told him she loved him and had him sit next to her on the couch, brushing his hair and giving him a neck massage until he fell asleep with his head in her lap. When his face relaxed into dreamless slumber, Delilah eased herself away from his heavy form. Stealthy as fog, she crept to an open window and gave the nightingale call. Within minutes, her cousin and his two coconspirators arrived.

"This time he told me the truth," she whispered. "I guarantee it."

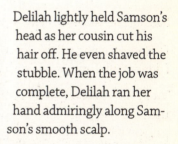

Delilah lightly held Samson's head as her cousin cut his hair off. He even shaved the stubble. When the job was complete, Delilah ran her hand admiringly along Samson's smooth scalp.

"Well done, cousin!" she whispered. At the sound of her voice, Samson began to stir. Delilah immediately grabbed his shirt and screamed.

"Help!" she cried. "Philistines!"

Samson jumped to his feet. This time there really were three Philistines! The three men surrounding the couch leered menacingly at him, swinging ropes and brandishing weapons. Unperturbed, Samson gave the first man a blistering right-left combination, the second a swift elbow to the throat, and the third a kick to the left kneecap. But the men fell back only half a step and were soon on him with renewed vigor.

Knocked off balance by a well-placed jab, Samson staggered and tripped over a throw pillow. He fell face-first into a pile of his own hair. Wide eyed, he seized two handfuls. Horrified, he felt his own naked head.

"Delilah!"

The three men jerked Samson from the carpet and tied him to a chair. As he was punched and manhandled, he searched the room for his love. She nonchalantly watched from the kitchen doorway.

"Why?" he pleaded.

She held up a bag of clanking coins and shrugged unapologetically. "Nothing personal, honey," she said. "Just business."

God Is Our Only Source of True Strength

God gave Samson superhuman strength with only a few conditions. One was that he was never to cut his hair.

Though Samson was a powerful warrior for Israel, his weak character turned out to be his ultimate undoing. He forgot where his real strength came from and betrayed the most precious gift he'd been given.

God doesn't give all of us record-breaking physical strength, but He does promise us the spiritual strength we need to get through any circumstance. All we have to do is ask.

More Great Harvest House Books
from Sandy Silverthorne

One-Minute Mysteries and Brain Teasers

The Awesome Book of One-Minute Mysteries and Brain Teasers

Mind-Boggling One-Minute Mysteries and Brain Teasers

Sandy Silverthorne and John Warner

These three books of short, interactive mysteries will provide hours of fun whether you solve them alone or challenge the sleuthing skills of your friends or family. Challenging enough for adults yet appropriate for detectives of all ages, each puzzle includes a cartoon that adds to the fun.

The Awesome Book of Unusual Bible Heroes for Kids
The Awesome Book of Bible Stories for Kids
101 Awesome Bible Facts for Kids
The Awesome Book of Bible Facts

Sandy Silverthorne

You'll love the interesting stories, entertaining cartoon drawings, and short, easy explanations packed into these four books.